CHRONIC PROFIT

CHRONIC PROFIT

Building Your Small Business
While Managing Persistent Pain

ALISON TEDFORD

Self-Counsel Press
(a division of)
International Self-Counsel Press Ltd.
Canada   USA

Self-Counsel Press acknowledges the financial support of the Government of Canada through the Canada Book Fund (CBF) for our publishing activities.

Self-Counsel Press gratefully acknowledges the Coast Salish, Tsleil-Waututh, Squamish, Sto:lo, Musqueam, and Nooksack peoples, on whose land our offices are located.

Printed in Canada.

First edition: 2021

Library and Archives Canada Cataloguing in Publication

Title: Chronic profit : building your small business while managing persistent pain / Alison Tedford.

Names: Tedford, Alison, author.

Series: Self-Counsel business series.

Description: 1st edition. | Series statement: Business series

Identifiers: Canadiana (print) 20210136014 | Canadiana (ebook) 2021013626X | ISBN 9781770403321 (softcover) | ISBN 9781770405226 (EPUB) | ISBN 9781770405233 (Kindle)

Subjects: LCSH: Entrepreneurship. | LCSH: Businesspeople—Health and hygiene. | LCSH: Chronic pain—Patients—Employment. | LCSH: Chronic pain—Psychological aspects. | LCSH: Businesspeople—Psychology. | LCSH: Work-life balance.

Classification: LCC HD62.5 .T43 2021 | DDC 338/.04—dc23

Self-Counsel Press
(a division of)
International Self-Counsel Press Ltd.

North Vancouver, BC	Bellingham, WA
Canada	USA

CONTENTS

NOTICE TO READERS

Laws are constantly changing. Every effort is made to keep this publication as current as possible. However, the author, the publisher, and the vendor of this book make no representations or warranties regarding the outcome or the use to which the information in this book is put and are not assuming any liability for any claims, losses, or damages arising out of the use of this book. The reader should not rely on the author or the publisher of this book for any professional advice. Please be sure that you have the most recent edition.

ACKNOWLEDGMENTS

Thank you to everyone who contributed their stories to my book; to my family for supporting me through this process (especially my mom, who lovingly transcribed every interview and my son who cheered for me); to Angela Crocker for believing in me; and to my brilliant editor.

PREFACE:
HOW AND WHY I'M HERE

"We can't let people keep dying out of politeness."

I wrote those words on May 7, 2020, on my Facebook page in frustration and devastation at another Black life lost. We were in the initial social isolation period everyone called quarantine and amidst the eerie quiet, Black people were still being killed by police and I had something to say about it.

I wasn't always loud like this in my business. I started my marketing practice without a specific point of view. It didn't have strong positioning in any respect other than that I created quality content, but over the course of quarantine I came into my own. I said what I felt needed to be said and it turned into both social change and client attraction.

Businesses were closing. People were crying and baking bread. I was a newly single mom, an entrepreneur with a struggling business that refused to give up. Corona took half my business the first week it hit, and I was devastated. I was worried I was going to become homeless. My long-term partner had just left and my business was imploding and I didn't know what the heck to do.

Going into that phase of the COVID-19 pandemic, I knew my life was never going to be the same because my family had dissolved, and it changed me. I was never going to be the same person that I was. And then all of a sudden, a virus ravaged Earth, and everybody was tossed into the same new lack of routine, lack of certainty, lack of anything that was familiar that I had become somewhat accustomed to over the course of a number of weeks.

So, I started sharing my deepest thoughts on Facebook under the hashtag #nofakebooking, and "we share the messages we need the most." I was something of a pandemic Pollyanna (I even bought the domain pandemicpollyanna.com) and I just started writing. I started pouring my heart out to the people who were in my world about the things that mattered to me. I wrote about Black lives. I wrote about Trans lives. I wrote about all of the things that were in my heart.

I started a community gratitude practice with daily check-ins where people would share about their days and how they were making it through.

My community and I bonded over the shared experience of a pandemic and how it affected our personal lives, our romantic lives, our business lives.

After all, it touched everything. But a funny thing happened. When it touched my life, everything grew. The chaos of this deadly virus and these horrible circumstances stabilized my business and made it grow. I was the calm, consistent, reassuring, hopeful but authentic voice my community needed to normalize what they were feeling. People got to know me — the real me.

I wrote a love letter to my community.

My Quarantine Life Project

I'm not planning to learn Spanish.

I won't be making sourdough.

I'm a copywriter. Every day I write things to convince people to buy the course, book the meeting, schedule the keynote, ditch the diets, make all sorts of changes.

I only sell things I believe in because I believe I'm good at what I do, and I only want to use it for good.

Words of Persuasion are my superpower.

My Quarantine Life project is to sell something a little different to you.

I'm determined to convince you to keep going (even though it's hard).

I want you to believe you're not alone (even if you're isolated).

I would love to see you exercise self-compassion and leave space for the big feelings (even when it's scary).

I would be so happy for you to feel validated and understand that whatever you're feeling right now is OK (even when it feels like a lot).

I want you to understand it's reasonable to not be OK, but I don't want it to overwhelm you completely (even when life gets really heavy).

I want to assure you that subscribing to diet culture will only make the space you have for joy smaller (even when people try to scare you about The Quarantine 15).

My goal is to keep showing up for you until you believe those things and until you buy into *you*, because I believe in you.

What is your quarantine life project?

I have immense survivor guilt about this: I know how many businesses didn't have the experience of thriving during a pandemic. But that was my experience. That was my truth. I lost almost everything in my business, and I stabilized it and I doubled my monthly pre-COVID revenue after so many years of going through the motions, keeping the lights on, and hoping something big would happen. A few months later it would triple.

I wanted my business to grow, but I didn't wish for the painful circumstances in which it ended up thriving.

After so many years of being behind the scenes, I became visible. I appeared on CBC Radio five times one day. I spoke on a panel about how to raise antiracist kids to hundreds of people. I was on global public radio about race-based data and Indigenous people and how they've been left behind by the healthcare system. I was on podcasts. I spoke anywhere people would listen and probably places people didn't.

I got really loud and people started paying attention. I also started listening really hard. I heard my fellow business owners complaining about how they didn't know how to talk to their communities about what was happening around them.

I watched icons get "cancelled" because of their ineffective responses to the Black Lives Matter movement. I saw people struggling with how to sell with sensitivity in a difficult time. People were confused, lost, and scared.

My natural instinct as a mom and nurturer was to comfort, to educate, and to reassure.

These questions that people had were all questions that I felt prepared to answer because of my extensive experience with intercultural communication in government, and my experience managing communities online, doing antiracism education to foster understanding and reduce systemic barriers. My experience as an Indigenous woman who has done all of these things had me perfectly positioned to be able to serve people who desperately needed serving.

When I tried to do antiracism education work informally while maintaining marketing practice, I found I was exhausted. Keeping those two pieces separate and maintaining them with the same level of fervor was depleting my already low energy.

After all, I was working really hard through the pandemic trying to keep the lights on and at the same time carrying an immense emotional weight trying to explain the experience of racism and I couldn't hold those two things separately. I needed to be able to bring them together in order to function. And that's how Stay Woke Not Broke, my first group program, was born.

My Story: In the Beginning

This is probably the most unexpected escape from prison story you will ever read, but here goes.

Entrepreneurship does not run in my family and as it turns out, I ran from the very thing my family always did, which was work in the prisons. I did a sixth grade project on substance abuse programming in the prison system and didn't think much of it. It was where my dad, my stepmom, my uncle, and my aunt worked. Later, my cousin, my stepbrother, and I would join also. It was what we did.

Looking back, I don't think I knew anybody who ran a business when I was growing up. This was so far outside of my plan it's almost laughable that I ended up here. Growing up I thought maybe I would become a lawyer or a psychologist, but things didn't turn out that way.

I thought my path was pretty much preordained when I got my first government job. I figured I had a career for life and the idea that I would be working from home designing national campaigns, working with brands and business owners all over the world, all from the comfort of my own living room never entered my mind.

I didn't have a degree in anything. I had a year of assorted college courses that together didn't amount to very much. I didn't feel like I had any of the ingredients to build a successful business. I didn't have a big idea. I just had a longing inside me to make something happen and I didn't even know what it was.

I wanted to change the world, but I didn't know where to start or if business could have anything to do with that. I didn't even have a business plan or a website or Facebook page. This never should have worked but it did.

A Good Dream, but Not My Dream (Leaving Government)

I started working in government when I was 18. I started in the Federal Treaty Negotiation Office doing clerical work and moved into working in the department that handled residential school claims where I would stay for a few years. Later I transferred to work in the prison system while I worked my way up from being a secretary to be a project officer specializing in Performance Measurement, Policy, Planning, Access to Information, and Privacy.

I had what so many people wanted, and I wasn't satisfied. I didn't feel like I had a lot of room for upward mobility when I got where I was at 32 and it was an uncomfortable feeling to feel like there wasn't much more than that for me to achieve. I felt stuck, like I peaked too early, and then what was I supposed to do?

I struggled with the antiquated Human Resources policies and internal hiring practices that made me jump through the same hoops over and over again to prove my disability and wait to see if my required accommodation would be honored.

Everybody connected to the process had the very best of intentions but there just wasn't a structure in place that made advancement as unencumbered as it is for people who don't have a disability. It felt so hard to get ahead and I was demoralized.

I struggled with long-term temporary opportunities that didn't translate to job security. Those situations meant that when the payroll system went haywire a large proportion of income could be at risk of not arriving. That wasn't a risk I was prepared to accept.

As the primary breadwinner in my home I needed to know that my money would arrive as scheduled in full. If I wasn't going to have that stability, I wanted the instability to be on my own terms.

Beyond the financial concerns, I found myself trying to solve the same problems over and over again and while there was progress it was discouraging and frustrating and a large ship to turn. I longed to work in a nimble organization that could easily implement strategic direction and change course with more ease than a government entity.

It's not that there was no desire for change, I worked with brilliant, kind, compassionate, amazing humans who wanted the very best. Nobody was nefariously opposing progress. But systems are hard to change. We were all people with the best of intentions trying to do the very best thing that we could within the constraints of what was possible. It just wasn't enough for me at the time.

When I joined the government, I was an idealist and I thought that I could change things from the inside and to be fair, I believe that a lot of the things that I did created meaningful change. I watched others do the same.

I just longed for something more. I didn't know what it was but there was something that didn't fit right. It was like wearing shoes that blistered my feet but looked really pretty. They looked nice, but it was so uncomfortable and painful inside.

I can't tell you how many hours I rehashed my discontent with friends who had varying levels of sympathy for my plight as I tried to figure out what life could look like. I wondered where I would have the satisfaction of achieving new things, of seeing meaningful change, and going to bed completely satisfied with my contribution to the world.

I actually wondered if that even existed. I wondered if I was just spoiled and selfish for not being happy with what so many people would love to have. So many people would tell me that, you know, "that's why it's called work" and for a lot of years I bought into that and I kept grinding, trying to find a way to be happy with something that wasn't appropriate for me.

I finally came to the realization that the work that I was doing could be a good dream, it could just be someone else's dream and that it didn't have to be bad for it not to be right. It could be a good thing for someone else and there could be something better for me.

It was the first time that I accepted that me not wanting to do something was reason enough not to do it. After so many years of being socialized to be accommodating and to do what I could if I could no matter whether I was interested in doing so or not, I felt it was time to honor my truth.

I tried to find small ways to explore what that could look like, a new life on the outside.

Falling in Love (with Blogging)

The first way I explored this possible new life was through blogging. Somebody at my gym suggested that I start blogging because my Facebook statuses were so funny. I didn't really think that it was going to work. I didn't think anyone would be interested in reading my posts. I figured maybe 12 people would read them and the blog would fade into obscurity, hopefully with very little embarrassment. But I decided to try, because what did I have to lose?

I started blogging about my feelings around equality, fitness, parenting, and mental health. I used it as my platform to talk about the things that were in my heart and the things that I was really passionate about like my local gym and the people that I met there and all of the fun adventures that I was going on as a single parent.

I made a lot of connections blogging and made great friendships. I was approached by brands fairly shortly after I started blogging and was asked to do sponsored content for them. This led to me being in an online commercial for my gym, doing a campaign for mental health awareness for a national drugstore chain, embarking on a partnership with a trampoline company, and even getting to look on as my son experienced the joy of becoming a Vancouver Canuck for a day.

I watched as he skated in Rogers Arena, accepted his jersey, signed a "contract" with the organization, and later he experienced a game from incredible seats. The most memorable moment of that experience was when Darcy Rota came up to him and greeted him by name. His eyes grew wide and he asked this famous hockey player "How did you know my name?" Darcy smiled at him and said, "It's taped to the front of your helmet."

I learned I had a voice and I learned some people actually cared what I had to say. I had social media channels that started to grow, and I started to learn through trial and error what worked, how to grow the channels, how to curate content that would interest people, and how to engage with and relationship-build with my audience.

I also learned about something called guest blogging. I learned that if you write for larger websites, people who read them will want to come over and read your blog and follow you on social media. My following grew and grew.

I started pitching publications with stories I could write for them. This expanded my network outside of Canada and into the US and ultimately worldwide as my content was accepted on collaborative blogs and in magazines. I got to make friends with and write with writers from all over the world. I traveled to Baltimore and met them.

Ultimately, my words would be accepted at the Good Men Project, Upworthy, Al-Jazeera, CBC, *Today's Parent*, *Asparagus Magazine*, To Write Love On Her Arms, Scary Mommy, Vancouver Mom, Urban Moms, *The Huffington Post*, *West Coast Families*, Savvy Mom, and more. My words got around the world. They were used in university classes. They became memes made by people I've never met.

I received thoughtful comments from people about how I was able to explain the things that they felt alone in feeling, that they didn't know other people felt that way, that they were inspired to keep going in the recovery from eating disorders or they felt less alone as a single parent. I wrote those words by myself, but they built community. My community.

My channels and influence grew and my writing skill improved and I learned how to work with editors, how to create content according to a pitch, how to pitch things, how to deal with criticism, how to approach difficult topics with authenticity and vulnerability, and how to really connect with people.

The idea of a writer in the cabin in the woods is not the reality of the modern writer. As much as it's about beautiful words and meaningful thoughts it's also about the power of connection and relationship-building. These are the things that help content get perfected, published, and shared.

My world got so big through the written word. I never expected how confident I would become through my writing and how many doors this would open for me.

The First Taste That Got Me Hooked (Subcontracting)

One door that would open for me was when the publisher of a blog that I wrote for, Bluntmoms, advertised that she had contract positions available in her marketing agency. I decided to throw my hat in the ring because I had experience building social media channels of my own so I thought maybe I could be useful in helping her build channels for her clients. She took a chance on me and I started with one Facebook account.

Over time, I grew the number of accounts for which I was responsible. I became part of her organization as a virtual assistant; I went from that one channel to realizing that this is what I wanted to do. I mean, not building Facebook pages specifically, but being independent and having my own business.

She was a corporate escapee like I wanted to be. She blew up her life and built something that she was really proud of and I really admired the way she approached business and life, and still do.

When I shared this longing and this secret desire to start my own business, she was so gracious. She introduced me to people who needed my services. She filled my funnel with new leads so that I could work full-time in my business. Over the course of five months I went from cubicle dweller to couch-based marketing consultant.

The first week I worked full-time in my business I was overwhelmed with the love and support that I received. She and her second-in-command were gracious enough to shower me with gifts including flowers, chocolates, a box full of items to help me manage my chronic pain when working from home, and a lap desk. I was so touched. My journey had begun in earnest.

I started with a three-month leave of absence to see if full-time entrepreneurship would be a fit for me. There came a point where I could not imagine returning and so I tendered my resignation.

Why I Became an Entrepreneur

Disillusioned by bureaucratic life I saw an opportunity to be creative and to be able to provide advice in a context where it could be immediately implemented, and I could see the results. I was able to see both the effects of long-term investment and instant gratification in working with people in my marketing practice.

I could pick and choose which projects I worked on, how much I would be paid for them, and I could make decisions as the head of my own entity that would position me for success, my definition of success.

I really craved creativity and the ability to innovate unencumbered by the trappings of bureaucracy. I wanted to build something all by myself and be proud of what I could accomplish. I wanted to prove to myself that I could do it and I wanted to see how far I could take it.

Unexplained Pain and Cubicle Life

The other reason that I pursued entrepreneurship was because of the pain that I was in. For years I experienced musculoskeletal pain with no rhyme or reason, seemingly. I was constantly nauseous. I struggled with panic attacks all day every day. I was hyper stimulated by an open office environment and needed quiet.

I didn't know why I was so sick, and I was nervous of pressing the issue with my care team. I expected that they would say that I was in discomfort because I was overweight, and I felt like there had to be more to it than that. I was afraid of being dismissed so I didn't push it until it became unbearable, long after I left.

I had been diagnosed with a number of conditions that were related to my ultimate diagnosis, which is Ehlers-Danlos Syndrome, and I struggled with navigating the work world while dealing with these issues.

Self-employment gave me what I needed before I knew why I needed it. I needed a space where I could accommodate myself without having to ask for anyone's permission. I needed to be able to nap when I needed to nap. I needed to be able to start my day when I felt ready and rested and well. I needed to be able to contort myself into whatever position was most comfortable regardless of how silly it looked.

I needed to be able to dress however I wanted to dress for the sake of my comfort. I had to constrain the length of my workday according to what I could tolerate on any given day and to be able to have the discretion to make that decision for myself.

I wanted less structure so that I could build something that works for me. I needed to be in the driver's seat of my career and to be able to pick and choose projects based on what works for me.

Ultimately, what I learned was that with my diagnosis stress is something that significantly impacts the severity of symptoms and so being able to select projects based on stress management was a game-changer for me.

My life living with this condition is not easy and I had to find ways to make it more bearable. I wanted complete control over my environment. I needed to be able to take control of my life in order to be able to take control of my wellness.

Craving Balance As a Mom

Another reason I decided to become an entrepreneur was so that I could be more involved as a mom. I wanted to be able to take days off to participate in field trips or things that were important to my son without having to worry if I could get the day off. It's not that time off was ever unreasonably denied, it's just that I didn't want to have to ask permission. I wanted flexibility to be a mom, to do what I do and to not have to worry about what people thought about that.

It turns out my son really enjoys me working from home and being an entrepreneur because he knows that when he needs me, I'm available and that I can be there for him. This proved particularly useful over the course of the pandemic when other parents were looking for childcare and trying to figure out how to navigate a world without school. We were already well-positioned because I was home and he could be home with me, and it was no problem.

I didn't have to worry about being limited by vacation time because I could work from wherever I am. I could bring my laptop and wake up early and work on things before we started out on touristy adventures. I could work anywhere with an internet connection or at least a cell phone signal. When my son's lacrosse tournaments started on a day that wasn't a weekend I could just work from the sidelines if necessary or from our hotel or in the car. I could have the freedom to make things work for me.

Longing for Flexibility

It's kind of funny because one of the hallmarks of Ehlers-Danlos Syndrome is hypermobility. By definition my body has too much flexibility, but I felt like my lifestyle wasn't flexible enough. I really needed the ability to work hard during some seasons, work less hard during other seasons, and to find balance in my own way.

I needed to be able to be creative about how I show up for people and how I serve my clients. I didn't want to be constrained by a job description. I wanted to write my own. I wanted to keep that under constant revision with each new experience assessing how things worked for me and whether projects were things I wanted to do more or less of.

I wanted to be able to grow what I wanted to grow at whatever speed I wanted to grow and just have room.

I longed for freedom. Like in that Dixie Chicks (now they go by "The Chicks") song, I needed "Wide Open Spaces." I needed "room to make her big mistakes" and boy did I make mistakes.

I'll tell you all about them in the following chapters.

1

THE EARLY DAYS: DON'T BUILD AN UNSUSTAINABLE BUSINESS LIKE I DID

I had no idea what I was doing when I started my business, and I made a lot of mistakes. I built something unwieldy, unmanageable, and completely unsustainable. It kept the lights on and provided for us but there were months where it was very tenuous. I was terrified a lot of the time and I was working so hard I thought my body would break.

But how did I get here? Wasn't this supposed to be my path to freedom and the way that I took care of my health? Wasn't this supposed to be the way that I built strong relationships with my family? Wasn't I supposed to be a better mom? Where did it all go wrong?

I asked myself that question a lot and while I didn't yet have all of the answers, I knew where I had gone wrong, ultimately, and what had led to the undoing and almost demise of my business.

I built it wrong with no plan and thankfully it survived, but this is what I learned which hopefully can help you not make the same mistakes that I did.

Too Many Offers

My business came together based on the pain points of the people in my circle. I listened to what entrepreneurs I knew were struggling with and if I knew how to do what they didn't enjoy doing then I would offer to do it.

As a result, I had an amazing number of offers. It was truly dizzying. While it meant that I was never bored, it was difficult to maintain.

I wasn't able to standardize how I approached things because everything was so custom and didn't have any structure to it that was standardized across my offers. I did social media management, email management, influencer marketing, freelance writing, content writing, graphic design, public relations, copywriting — almost anything anybody would ask, I would do just to make sure that we were keeping the lights on at home.

Beyond the fact that it was difficult to do so many different things for so many different people, the other issue was that I wasn't really known for anything. I was a jack-of-all-trades, master of none.

Some might call that a full-stack marketer, but I call it a full headache. I wasn't standing out in any way. I was barely standing at all.

I wasn't known for things except for my writing ability. I was doing too many things and that made it difficult for people to refer other people to me appropriately. They didn't know where to start. It was like having a Cheesecake Factory menu as a Services list.

Because I wasn't specialized, I wasn't able to charge premium rates for my services and it was difficult to create consistent messaging around what I do and how people work with me. The answer was very ambiguous: It depends. I would do anything for anybody, at a range of prices, and it was exhausting.

Decision fatigue was setting in because I had so many things that I was juggling in so many different ways and had so many conflicting deadlines. My offers were so small that I had to make things up in volume which meant I was working myself to the bone, exhausted and overwhelmed.

When you do the same thing in the same way you can create repeatable processes that save time. But when you have a mishmash of things it's hard to be able to create processes so that you can deliver services consistently every single time, especially when you are a solopreneur. It also makes it really hard to delegate because the instructions are different for every single thing and there isn't a standard operating procedure and way of handling things. There can be overarching philosophies but in terms of consistent policy application it can be really difficult when you have too many offers.

The other thing is that when you have such a big list it can be overwhelming for customers or clients, and overwhelmed or confused people tend not to buy. Too many options can make a choice difficult.

When you have too many offers it can be hard to keep track of everything on days when you have lots of pain like I often do, or when you have brain fog. You have to rely on a lot of external cues and the way of being in your business is less intuitive.

Creating an elevator pitch for what you do can be really challenging when you have too many services because it's difficult to succinctly describe what it is that you do. It's a bit easier when the things that you do fall into logical buckets and groupings, but it is much simpler when what you do can be easily understood by your target audience and that ease can lead to more sales and higher value sales.

Weak Policies

Something I learned the hard way was that I had to structure my policies in consideration of the target audience and how they operate and how they interact with my services.

For example, initially, I allowed for pay-as-you-go services which made it difficult to manage my inventory, which was my time.

When you provide services on an hourly basis and let people use them on a pay-as-you-go basis, then you don't know how many hours you'll be asked to work and if somebody asks for a specific number of hours but only pays for the portion that they actually use, you've reserved time on your calendar that they're not paying for and no one else is either.

Not having control of your inventory leaves you in the unenviable position of needing to oversell your hours in order to pay the bills. This is incredibly problematic if everybody uses the number of hours they said they needed, when they don't normally use them, and then you need to work overtime in order to make sure everybody is happy. You won't get any sleep.

You really do need to have inventory control in place to make sure that you're not in the position of either scrambling at the end of the month to make bank or scrambling to stay awake to make, package, or otherwise do the things that you sold because people are actually using what they said they would use.

It's really important to understand your client demographic to be able to gauge the likelihood of each scenario. A lot of times people will hire a virtual assistant or another type of service with the intention of using the service, but they don't. It's like buying an agenda you never write in. You can't always rely on clients to be motivated enough to use the services that they requested if there's no financial incentive for them to do so.

Having weak policies that don't compensate you for setting aside time is a good way to get in a bad way with your bank account, self-care, hours of work, relationships, and business growth. Time is your most precious resource and you need to be able to account for it so that you know how much time you have left to sell and so that you can prioritize tasks appropriately. You don't want to end up with a month of work and everything scrunched in at the end of your month.

Likewise, it's important to put boundaries around how long hours can be carried forward. Your circumstances could change in the future and you need to be able to protect yourself so that you're not over committed on hours purchased months ago.

You also need to be able to have control over your time and know how much time you have left to sell to new clients. Having too many prepaid hours with no limit on when they can be used is a liability. It means you can't guarantee quality if you're overworking and exhausted and needing to deliver things because everyone's calling in their hours at the same time.

Set strong policies that work for you and the way your target audience will work with you.

No Self-care

I assumed, when I started my business, I would be able to be so focused on my wellness and fitness and that I would be a healthy, balanced person because I would have the time and flexibility to do that.

Spoiler: That's not what happened. That's the furthest thing from what happened.

It turns out that if you want to have self-care then you need to schedule time for it and you need to have policies, procedures, and office hours in place so that you get the time that you need to take care of yourself. It isn't enough to have the time to be able to do something, you have to actually prioritize it and make sure it happens. Having the capacity to do something is different than actually doing something — having a plan to do something and accountability in place to make sure that you follow through.

Trying to work on not enough rest, not enough food, not enough fluids, not enough free time can be detrimental to your business. It leaves you short with clients, patience, inspiration, and in your ability to enjoy your time off.

As a business owner you are your biggest business asset. It is what makes you money. You need to take care of yourself. If you had a laptop that made you money, you wouldn't tie it to your bumper and drive it through town. You would put that in a case and keep it safe so that it doesn't get run over.

You need to treat your body in the same way otherwise you will end up with a body that doesn't support the business that you want to build. You will end up not well enough to participate in what you've built.

Self-care helps you build resilience and helps you weather the storm of entrepreneurship. Building a business can be stressful and you need to be able to have the resources available to you to manage that stress, and that comes from taking care of yourself.

When you work too long without enough breaks, when you don't resource your body with the food or the fluids that it needs, when you don't take time for yourself, you are writing checks your body can't cash. This is particularly true for anyone with a chronic health condition.

In the early days, I didn't take care of myself. I didn't make sure that I was eating appropriately or often enough. I wasn't feeding my body with the right foods at the right time and the right amount. I wasn't drinking enough water so I was dehydrated and cranky. I wasn't sleeping enough, and I was cranky with clients and with my family and I wasn't able to focus because I was so tired.

My best work comes when I take care of myself. When I take care of myself, I can take care of my clients and my family. When I take care of myself, I can take care of my responsibilities and deliver on my promises.

That's the whole reason I did this. I built a business so I could take care of myself and I needed to actually do it.

When I realized how much I had failed in my self-care I realized how unsustainable my business was, because my business is no more sustainable than my capacity to participate in it. I knew I had to turn it around. That's when I decided I needed to go see my doctor and figure out what was going on with my body.

Seek a Diagnosis If You Need One

The time that passed from when I went to the doctor to finally ask for help, to when I saw the rheumatologist and got my diagnosis was about four months. It felt like forever. I went through test after test so that when I saw the specialist, they would be able to better understand what was going on.

I was really nervous and didn't know what to expect. I had never been to a rheumatologist before and I didn't know if the problem was in my joints, and part of me second-guessed whether I was just too heavy and maybe that was the issue causing so much body pain.

When I was finally diagnosed, I was underwhelmed in some ways. I thought that when they knew what was wrong with me, they could fix me. It never even occurred to me that there would be something wrong that nobody could fix. I was not prepared for the answer to be "take better care of yourself, try not to be stressed, sleep more, try to be more mobile," and pain management.

The thing about having a systemic condition that affects your whole body is that all of a sudden you have context for things you couldn't explain before. It's like finding the box that goes with a puzzle and you can finally see where the pieces are supposed to go and what it all means when it gets put together. Those moments of realization come in spurts, like gushes coming out of a faucet.

It can be really validating in some ways to have an explanation for the way that you're feeling. All of a sudden everything makes sense, and it wasn't all in your head: It was real. For so many years I felt like a hypochondriac and that there was no possible way so many different things were wrong with me, but it turns out there was just one big thing that was wrong with me that caused all sorts of other things to be wrong and I finally felt less crazy.

The fact that I would be diagnosed with something for which there's no cure and really not much in the way of treatment was something that never even crossed my mind. I just assumed it would be like it is on *House* where they would be able to treat and fix me and then send me home. The truth of the matter was a lot more complicated.

Grieving While Running a Business

When I finally realized what was wrong and there wasn't a lot that could be done about it, I was so angry. I felt cheated and ripped off. I watched the life I thought I could have slip through my swollen, dislocated fingertips.

I was grieving the fact that having more kids was not recommended; that I couldn't operate in the same full tilt 24/7 way that I had been used to and that there was a legitimate medical reason that would require me to slow down. I thought that was a limiting factor.

I went through this bargaining phase where I thought, maybe if I work really hard for a few years then I can slow down and do what the doctor said. And in effect, that's what happened. Not medically recommended, but that's the reality.

I was angry that I had so much pain and I couldn't get relief. I thought it was unfair and, as someone with a strong sense of justice, I couldn't sit with this feeling that I had been treated unjustly by my own body. I felt betrayed by my body.

I focused on what my body could do and now my body couldn't do the things it used to do. I had to learn how to find my own sense of worth that didn't lie in productivity in a traditional sense.

I had been a card-carrying member of hustle culture and this diagnosis revoked my card. I no longer had privileges to run amok until the wee hours of the morning in order to meet deadlines. My body just wasn't built for this.

Most of all, I felt alone. I had to find other people like me.

Find Community and Connection to Conquer

The diagnosis brought some comfort at least. I knew what I was dealing with and I would be able to find other people like me. I had always been somebody who trusted in science and believed that anecdotal evidence was unreliable. Unfortunately, when you are dealing with a rare disease, anecdotes are a big piece of what you have to work with.

Part of gathering those anecdotes is meeting the people who have those stories to tell.

People with Ehlers-Danlos Syndrome (EDS), the condition I have, are often referred to as zebras, and the collective noun for zebras is a dazzle. They call us that because of the old expression, "When you hear hoof beats, think horses, not zebras." Connective tissue disorders like mine are rarely diagnosed because doctors attribute symptoms to the simplest explanation and rarely think it could be a systemic problem such as EDS. I had to find my dazzle. I needed to find zebras like me so that I could understand what I was going through better.

The validation that came from finding people like me was unparalleled. Their stories gave me answers science could not. I didn't feel like I was the only one anymore and that was so comforting. I really needed that sense of community because chronic pain and long-term illness can be so isolating.

I started with social media. I found people using a hashtag of my condition. I started sharing about it on Facebook and friends I didn't know had the condition started coming forward and saying, "Hey, I've got that too!" Their support was remarkable. I really needed to see examples of other people living successfully with my condition.

I connected with the Ehlers-Danlos Society and participated in what they called an ECHO, which was a group that educated patients to become advocates. I got to learn from experts in my disease and I was able to ask questions that I never thought I would be able to ask.

After the rheumatologist diagnosed me, he provided care instructions to my primary care physician and that was the end of his involvement with my case. I felt like I didn't have a connection to a medical professional who truly understood and specialized in my condition. It's not that he could do anything but it's just after that initial appointment I did more research and I had more questions, but I didn't have anybody to ask.

The reality is that when you get diagnosed with a chronic condition like this late in life, there are so many things that you were used to and accepted as normal that you wouldn't think to bring up to a doctor because that's just how you've always lived your life. You don't know that it's not normal. You wonder if he or she knew that information, if his or her advice would be different.

I didn't know anything about this condition when I walked into the appointment and I didn't know to what extent the things that I was experiencing related to that. I was diagnosed in-office and walked out with the knowledge that my life would be different if I followed my doctor's advice, and that the things that I accepted as being part of living life were actually symptoms of something that was wrong. It provided a whole different context for my experiences.

In the absence of an ongoing relationship with a healthcare provider who could give me more information about what I was going through I found that the support of my Ehlers-Danlos patient community was crucial. Everyone needs somewhere they're not considered to be weird.

When you have a condition that doesn't have a cure or a prescribed treatment regimen, when you talk to people about it, it's almost like you have to comfort them and reassure them it's okay because they feel so sad. When you're already emotionally depleted that can take a lot of effort emotionally. It's so helpful to have people who understand what you're going through because they've been through it too and you don't have to take care of them when you're talking about your experiences, you can just share.

The value of community became even more apparent to me as we went through the pandemic. A month or two before COVID-19, in the "before," my neighbor and I sat up late messaging like we do sometimes solving the problems of the world and we were talking about social connection and the difference between proximity and closeness.

The principle we discussed was that proximity is a bunch of beads in a jar and when you take the jar away the beads scatter. Closeness is when the beads are woven together and when the jar is removed, the beaded bracelet remains, securely attached.

I came to realize some of the sadness we were experiencing is that the containers that once gave us proximity (work, school), which had the illusion of closeness, were taken away with physical distancing. In addition to grief and loss of actual relationships and connection, we were also grieving the loss of the illusion of those things. In what felt like the absence of community I found the truth of what it was and what it really meant and why it matters so intensely for people like me.

Don't Give in to the Self-Doubt

When I was diagnosed, I just felt this deep loss of potential. I felt like I could expect less of life. I didn't have a mental map for a successful entrepreneur with a disability and I didn't know if I could still have it all. I finally had this business and it felt like the rug had been pulled out from under me.

I started to doubt whether I could be successful. I wondered if this meant I couldn't run a business. I was afraid that I couldn't do it. Before, when I thought I just wasn't trying hard enough, it felt like something I could overcome with motivation. But when I had to admit that there's a physically limiting issue and a physiological reason why certain things were just not possible; I was ready to give up.

I laid on my sofa and thought, "There's no way I can do this. I can't do this. I quit." I tender my resignation to my business all the time. It's a good thing my boss doesn't take it seriously. (It's a good thing my boss is me.)

I was so afraid that I couldn't do this. I was so afraid I was going to fail and end up homeless. I was scared I couldn't provide for my kid. I wondered if I had value from a potential partner's perspective. I worried how long I would be able to support myself. I was full of self-doubt just like I was full of inflammation. At least with inflammation I could ice things or elevate or rest but with self-doubt the only antidote seems to be to keep going because giving up wasn't an option either. I thought I couldn't do it because I couldn't work long days like other people. I thought I couldn't do it because my energy level wasn't the same. I worried I wasn't going to be competitive because other people could work longer and harder than I could.

I feared that people would not take me seriously or trust me when they knew that there was something wrong with me. I was nervous when people found out that they would see me as too fragile and they would not think I was strong enough to do what I need to do.

My condition is progressive, and I worried that it would accelerate and leave me unable to participate in my business. I was used to working under stress and I didn't know if I could find situations that were not stressful.

My body desperately needed a break from the stress, and I wondered if stress was just part of business and if this is all I could expect from life. I worried my inability to tolerate stress from a physical perspective meant that I, as a person, was weak.

I realized I couldn't work longer but I could work smarter. I realized that where I could not do what others could do, I had the opportunity to find different ways of doing things. I was no longer constrained by having to do things the way they've always been done because my body couldn't do those things. I had to find a new way to interact, to build my business, to exist as a businesswoman that wasn't so mired in tension.

I realized that the empathy that my condition cultivated within me made me able to create content that was intensely relatable. It made me highly competitive in my industry because I have the gift of being able to take someone else's perspective, because I know what pain is like. I considered the problem solving that I had to undertake to retrofit my home to fit my medical needs, and saw how I could use that same spirit of innovation to better serve clients. I learned that the perseverance that I had within me to withstand life with this condition meant I was uniquely positioned as an entrepreneur because I have grit and determination to get through the most difficult of circumstances where there seems to be no reprieve.

The sense of hopefulness that I possess because I remain optimistic despite facing very difficult odds means that I am able to encourage and believe in my customers so much more because I've had to practice that with myself. I'm an exceptional cheerleader for the people in my circle because I have had to cheer myself on through completely disappointing circumstances.

I can't do things other people can do but I can do things my way and that is enough. I bring a unique perspective to the business world because of what I have been through and I have lots to offer because of that. I have an additional lens through which I can view the world and that is of a person with a disability. I can offer feedback and consult on issues because of my lived experiences, and so can you.

2
SIMPLIFY YOUR BUSINESS

When you are dealing with chronic pain, complications are a medical fact of life. They don't have to be a fact of life professionally, though. It might be time to uncomplicate your business. If it all feels like too much, you might be doing too much.

The KISS rule is so important with chronic pain. "Keep It Simple, Silly," of course. Why make it harder when you're symptomatic? There is no prize for the most complicated business. Complications just add to stress and in many cases additional stress means additional pain. This is why simplicity is so important.

It's also about setting things up for the worst case scenario. Sure, complicated things can be executed accurately when you're feeling well. But when you're not feeling well, complications are additional stressors that you don't need in your life. Chronic pain symptoms make complicated businesses even more complicated. It's a lot to keep track of and takes up a lot of mental space and when you are dealing with pain, your mental space is limited.

When you get to a point where you feel like maybe you're doing too many things it's important to take a pause and take stock of what you are doing, what you want to do, and how you want to work. I always tell people that you can answer the phone at a spa or for 911, either way it comes down to what you want to do with your life. It comes down to how you want to experience your work and whether you are the type who thrives under pressure or the type who enjoys the luxury of taking your time.

Are You Doing Too Many Things?

You might be asking yourself how to tell if you're doing too many things. Melissa Rodgers, business coach at Self-Made Mama explains.

"You can't stop thinking about your work and not in a good way. Typically, I'm always thinking about my business, but in a happy way. I'm getting excited about it. But there have been times, and there continue to be times, where I let things creep in a little bit too much, or I take on too much. Then I can't stop thinking about it in a stressed-out way."

It's not just how you feel about work but also how you feel about yourself. Melissa continues, "Every time I'm with my kids, or every time I'm trying to sleep or doing anything that isn't working, I feel guilt and stress."

That stress can cause problems. Melissa elaborates, "Usually that stress physically manifests and particularly if you are dealing with a health issue, that physical manifestation happens a lot faster than it does in a perfectly healthy body. Anytime you're compromised at all, that physical manifestation of your stress is going to be quite acute."

How about that attention span? When you're overwhelmed it can be the first thing to go. Melissa described it like this: "You're struggling to focus. When you have too many little things going on all at once, and you have no idea what you're supposed to do when you sit down to work, then you're not making enough progress and you're just compounding your own stress. You feel like you're always working and never getting anything done. That's a big sign that things are too complicated."

You might feel alone in feeling that way, but you're not, Melissa reassures us. "That's an inevitable place to get to as an entrepreneur, at least within your first couple years, depending on how fast your business grows. It's almost like you start your business journey and you're expanding, and you're expanding, you're expanding, and all of a sudden, you hit this wall, 'I'm doing too much. This isn't fun anymore.' Then you have to contract again. I do feel like that is a necessary progression. As a solopreneur, at least, that's a necessary evolution, because you have to hit that wall to realize what the things are that you want to cut away."

Streamline Your Offers

The easiest way to cut away is to streamline your offers. Hilary Jastram, author of *Sick Biz* (Sound Wisdom, 2018), explained how she realized that she needed to streamline.

"Somebody said to me, 'I looked at your website, and you do everything. I don't know what you do. I don't know who you are, and I don't know what your expertise is.' And that day, I cut five services."

Hilary decided, "From this day forward I will only do copyediting, copywriting, and book editing. And that's it, anything else will be outsourced."

Bite-Sized Business course creator and founder of The Reinvention Co, Dusti Arab agrees with this approach.

"As far as offer design goes, the more specific you can get the better."

Briar Harvey, online business strategist concurs, suggesting, "Pick one thing and do it well for a while. When you have chronic pain, in particular, you are not going to see your results from chasing shiny objects. Pick one thing, drill down until it's making money, then automate it. Pick one audience, one thing to sell, and keep doing that until you are selling it."

But how do you pick the one thing? Melissa Rodgers offers this advice. "My favorite way to teach people is to boil it down to a promise. What can you promise your dream client? Your dream client is somebody that the problem that you solve is their priority, or at least one of their top priorities and it is somebody that has the funds to invest in you at the price point that you have determined. It's somebody that highly values the promise that you are making."

She explains why that particular choice of words is so important. "Because we're using the language of promise, it has to be something that you feel competent delivering. That doesn't mean that you're responsible for the client's results or the customer's results. But you are responsible for delivering on the promise that you're making."

You might wonder what doing one thing looks like at various stages of your business. Melissa offers, "I like to fan it out into two or three tiers. A lot of people prefer a one-offer approach. If you just have one single offer, then that's how you're going to make the most money in your business. I think for beginner entrepreneurs, the first three or four years, I think it's crucial to have tiers of service available, because not everybody that is a dream client is going to be confident to jump in at your highest price point."

Just because clients start at your lowest tier doesn't mean that's where they will stay. Melissa shares her experience, "I would say that the majority of my clients have started with me at a lower price point, and very quickly scaled up to become key high-ticket clients. That's been really crucial in my business."

She talks about how she implemented the one promise principle in her business, "I promise that I will help you create consistent full-time income, essentially, over time. Obviously, I can't guarantee that you're going to make full-time income every month because you're a person and you're going to do whatever you're going to do. But I can give you all the resources, tools, and support that you need to do so."

She uses a tiered approach to deliver on that promise and she explains what that looks like on a practical level.

"You can work with me one on one, in an intensive coaching experience, that's my highest tier, you can join my group coaching, that's my middle tier, or you can purchase a small self-study program, that would be the bottom tier with no access to me."

Tiers benefit the consumer and the service provider. Melissa says, "This allows different kinds of buyers to purchase from you. You're still only offering one thing. Because your lower tiers are just pieces of your high tier, it's not more work for you. It's not context switching, which is huge when it comes to simplifying your business. But it's still offering a variety because people psychologically like to feel in control of their buying decision and offering them those tiers gives them control."

Standardize Your Offers

Just like in streamlining, there are signs your offer needs to be standardized. This was a big struggle that I faced, like I mentioned, during the pandemic because everything was so custom, and it became a lot to track.

I asked Melissa Rodgers how to tell if you need to standardize your offers. She responded, "A big [sign] would be every single or the majority of people that you get on a sales call with, or that make inquiries, are wanting to customize what you're offering."

That compulsion to customize comes from somewhere. Melissa talks about why buyers do that. "People feel confusion around your offer, or if people are unsure about how what you've laid out is actually going to serve them, their instinct is going to be to try and control the offer and to tailor-make something for themselves."

But why does that happen? Melissa explains, "That's an indication of two things: one, that your offers are confusing and they're not standardized enough, but also that you are bringing people into your world that are not aligned with your offers, which is a form of simplification that is very important."

The result of that lack of alignment can get messy and for good reason. Melissa describes it like this: "People come in and they'll start saying "Well, can you do just this part of this, can you add this?' Then you're doing everything à la carte. Because you made everything so complicated that nobody knows what they actually need from you."

Be Clear about Who Your Customer Is

When you're clear about who you're selling to, the sales process just gets easier. When I refined my ideal client avatar, I was able to make sales more easily and deliver their services more easily.

Melissa Rodgers warned of a sign you need to streamline who you sell to more thoroughly, "You're constantly getting price objections. Ninety percent of the people that you are actually talking to one on one about your services should be a yes. That's when you know that things are actually aligned."

Regardless of how you streamline your target market, you need to pick people who have a budget for what you do, Melissa cautions. "The majority of the time you want to make sure that people that you're interacting with, that are making inquiries are, people that are already ready to invest in you, they just have, almost, housekeeping questions."

Alignment doesn't mean that every single sale will be a walk in the park. Melissa says, "Maybe they might have a little bit of fear that you need to dissuade just by providing confirmation about outcomes and timelines and things like that. There are all different kinds of buyers. But you can have three or four different kinds of buyers that are all your dream clients, that are all your aligned clients, but they just need different things to push them to that close."

Avoid Scarcity Mindset when Limiting Your Scope

Limiting your scope can feel scary. Turning down money when you're trying to make money and feeling like you don't have enough money is overwhelming at times. It's so hard to say no when people want to give you money but sometimes you have to in order to better position yourself and not leave yourself so stretched.

Hilary Jastram explained, "Scarcity mindset is the fear of what might happen. But if you remain in control as much as you can and keep working towards things ... you can take the scarcity mindset away. You ensure that you're going to be OK, because you're going to do the work to fill its place."

In addition to hard work, it's important to keep a positive mind-set about the size of your market and your potential sales. Dusti Arab shared her affirmation to bust scarcity, "There's so many more people out there that I can serve who need what I have."

Guide and Big Black Tea founder Tim Salau, who is also known as Mr. Future of Work, offered this encouragement: "If you're creating something that inspires people, that keeps people elated, that people want to tell other people about, that people feel is a vitamin in addition to really solving a problem, you'll have no problem selling your product, you'll have no problem finding customers."

While you might be limiting to whom you sell, Tim believes the market has so much room and urges entrepreneurs to keep going. "There are 7 billion people in the world. And by 2035 there will be around 8.5 billion. So, there's someone out there that can be a potential customer. There are probably thousands to millions of people, but as an entrepreneur you can't give up."

Melissa Rodgers thinks it's important to acknowledge that while scarcity is a mindset that we want to avoid, there is literal scarcity that entrepreneurs sometimes contend with and that can be a whole other problem.

"I think that we're so hard on that, that sometimes people get a little bit ashamed of feeling scarce. I live in a very expensive part of the world. Your average person getting started making a few thousand dollars a month from their freelancing or from their business, whatever it is, that's not going very far. So, you may be making consistent sales, and you may be really killing it in your business, because to have consistent sales in the first couple years in your business is such an amazing milestone. But you may feel scarc[ity] because your bank account is still drained regularly, and all the time."

So, what do you do when scarcity, real or imagined, rears its head? Melissa's advised, "I think you have to acknowledge that you have to just be okay with the fact that those feelings come up and that they're normal. It's really important that you name them. I acknowledge them and I think through them."

Why is scarcity a problem? Melissa explained what happens when you feel scarce: "You'll behave in a desperate manner. You'll take clients that you shouldn't take, you'll try to scramble for sales that you really shouldn't be scrambling for. The result will be that you are now burned out from your overcomplicated business where you're unable to deliver. So, you're working with unideal clients, you're closing on unideal projects, and then you're unable to deliver because you stress yourself out so much that your body is now reacting."

She explains the problem with that reaction. "You are perpetuating this cycle for yourself, where the reality is that we can control our thoughts." Instead, she suggests, "When you're facing a circumstance of scarcity, or perceived scarcity, you have to train yourself, consciously choose another thought."

When Melissa feels scarce, she uses mental tricks to get over it. "My favorite trick is actually to look at the days that are left in the month. And it doesn't matter if there are 25 days or 5 days, I say, 'I have 20 days left to make all the sales that I want to make. There are a whole 5 days left in the month; the month is not over yet.'"

Having a booming business doesn't make you immune to scarcity, so don't beat yourself up if you're struggling with it. Melissa still deals with scarcity even in a successful business. She shared, "As someone who lived paycheck to paycheck for so long, that first of the month, when all the big bills are due, still brings up a little bit of anxiety for me, and I have to push myself through that. The earlier you start doing that, the more successful you'll be."

Find the Riches in the Niches

Focusing on one specific niche is a common tactic as part of streamlining, and while it might feel like you're saying no to money, you can actually use niching as a way to call in more money. Dusti Arab explained, "having that really clear in the marketplace has made it much easier to find clients."

The process of "niching" is to focus your business on specific industries or services. The idea is to get really clear on who you want to serve and how so that you can more easily market your services and more quickly become known as an expert in your field.

Cat Stancik, lead generation expert explains the anxiety around niching and why it's something to push through. "People are afraid to niche down because of the scarcity, it's a lack mindset. 'If I get narrow, I leave all of this off the table.' The problem is if you don't niche down, you can't even get to the table. You're standing in the crowd in the back."

There is a lot of confusion about what niching actually involves also, Cat clarifies, "A lot of people focus on the psychographics and demographics. What I want to invite people to do is look at values. The niche will present itself to you once you understand who you really want to work with over and over and over and over again."

But how do you push past it? Melissa Rodgers offers her advice, "For me, at least it's been more of a leap of faith. I've had to close my eyes and grit my teeth and say 'no.' Saying 'no' is not something that comes easily to a lot of people. Much the same way that you have to prioritize, and sometimes say 'no,' even when something is a priority, in order to take care of yourself or in order to manage, it's the same with your business. You can't operate in your business by saying yes to everyone and everything."

Once you start niching, there's a temptation to go back because of fears of leaving money on the table and because people will want to work with you who aren't in your niche. Melissa encourages restraint, suggesting, "You have to remind yourself that you have to leave room for the right things to come in. You have a capacity, and everyone has a different capacity. If you're dealing with a flare up, or you're dealing with a health issue, your capacity is even more limited. You have to leave room for the stuff that you actually want. Because if you fill your bucket with crap, there's no space left."

Be a specialist rather than a generalist

Niching and specializing lets you lean into being an authority in your field. Hilary Jastram explains the power of specializing and establishing yourself as a thought leader in the area you prefer to work.

"It actually speeds up the process of somebody saying, 'You've been doing this for so long, you must know what you're doing. I'm going to go to you because you've also demonstrated commitment to very specialized areas.' That's important for prospects and your clients, 'Well, this is all she does. So, I'm going to go there.'"

Specializing in a key area opens up more opportunities to be featured in interviews, because you are the expert. That increased visibility can help you gain more clients and can help you gain valuable search engine optimization with link backs in published articles. When you specialize you can charge more because you know more.

Starting out as a generalist can be helpful to let you experiment with the kinds of work that you like to do and find the kinds of people you like to work with and the problems you want to solve. Once you figure out what it is that you want to do, leaning into that can position you more effectively and help you close more deals.

3
BUILD SYSTEMS AND PROCESSES

Systems are the best friend of a business owner, especially one who has chronic pain, for so many reasons. Systems can help you stay on track, grow, and cope with the realities of daily pain.

I asked Amber Ingraham, Business Launch Engineer, international best-selling author and leader of The Biz Launch Code, who struggles with chronic pain, whether she would do things differently if she could go back to when she first started her business. She answered, "I would have more systems in place for sure to keep me more consistent. Because in the beginning, it was very touch and go with all of the pain, dealing with all of those things that get affected when you're not feeling well."

When you don't have a system, you have to think about it each time how you're going to execute something. That isn't anything you want to deal with when you feel terrible. Sharon Benson, Certified Online Business Manager Trainer, says, "Systems are the foundation of a business. If you don't have that foundation built, the whole house is going to crumble. You can have a business just on sheer luck and make six figures and you're doing it all yourself and that's great. But at some point, you're going to crumble because you don't have that foundation and the system set up. You can't have a strong business that you can leverage and grow with, unless you have that foundation set up."

You can't just hire a team and think you don't need systems because you have people. Tina Forsyth, Online Business Manager trainer, says, "You can hire a team, but without systems, your risk the work being done incorrectly, which can lead to a cycle of 'this didn't get done right, so I'm going to take it all back.'"

But where do you start with implementing systems? Tina recommends, "Anything lather, rinse, repeat. Anything that needs to be done once — daily, weekly, or monthly — is ripe to have a system built around it. With systems in place, we don't have to be involved in doing the work anymore."

Because the truth is, we don't have to do it all ourselves. People can help us.

She points to her own experience in delegating to explain how it's possible through systems. "The very first hire I ever made was a virtual assistant who started sending my newsletter out for me. I put a template together, built in a process, and trained her how to do it. Because we did that with the systems, then she could do it as well as me. If we hadn't built out the system, chances are she wouldn't have done it right, and I would have found myself in a dangerous loop of thinking, 'I tried hiring someone but It didn't work out, so I'm going to take it all back and keep doing it myself.'"

She also sees it as a way to dial in on your zone of genius. "Most of us got in business to do something we enjoy doing — our zone of genius. It's important to protect our time and energy, and make sure we don't get caught up in doing too many things outside our zone of genius."

Teri Holland, high-performance coach, agrees, "One thing I coach my clients on to keep in mind is what do you love doing in the business? When I was in personal training, a common thing was that a trainer, when they went to level up the business, would hire other trainers underneath them. They'd open a gym and then they weren't happy because they weren't doing the thing they love, which is working with people, they were in a management role." Delegating the wrong thing can actually bump you out of your zone of genius if you're not careful.

Jake Schaap, a business coach who works with clients who have autoimmune conditions, says, "If you want to create a repeatable process that you can eventually offload either on to someone else on your team that you bring on or just that you automate and get it off your plate, you have to have some sort of a system/formula/ framework in place that is repeatable, because not only will that alleviate stress and decision fatigue, it also just benefits your business as a whole."

He talks about that in terms of credibility and profitability, explaining, "That gives you more credibility as a business because you have a proven system that you can jack up the price for because you have that system in place. You're basically productizing your service if you are offering a service."

Systems are a way of harnessing habits to carry you through tough times. You can lean into your systems when you don't have the energy to think about things. You just follow your systems. They also allow you to have quality control and ensure consistency because when you follow a system, you are achieving results through the same methodology time after time. That's something you can become known for and being known for something is a great way to call in more clients.

System Types

Automation is a type of system that helps you execute your work. Amber Ingraham talked about how she leveraged automation in her business and why it was so important. "Consistency-wise, I found that I really need systems to help with scheduling posts and stuff so that if I'm not feeling it that day and not feeling well, it just auto does it. I take on a lot less one-on-one stuff, and more automated stuff so that I'm not physically having to be present all the time."

Frameworks are another way to use systems to execute your work. Frameworks can act as decision trees that guide your process. They are guiding principles and components of your proven method that standardize what you deliver. Business coach Rachel Rogers advocates for a framework methodology in her best-selling program Glow Up. She encourages clients to create frameworks to standardize their offers and the way they talk about them. Rachel Rodgers believes that this allows you to differentiate your service through a signature offer that is easy to explain.

Policies are a system too. They are a system for how work is completed, how customer inquiries are handled, and how your business runs. When you have policies in place, you can apply them to inquiries and spend less time thinking through each request. It's a shortcut for customer service and it allows you to create consistency in the way customers are treated.

Documenting Your Systems

It's not enough to have systems, you also have to document them. Documentation is key to ensuring that systems are followed and implemented as imagined. That documentation can be helpful for outsourcing and for ensuring that you follow your own processes.

Keldie Jamieson, Certified Online Business Manager Trainer, suggests starting to document as follows. "Start a foundational asset book, or spreadsheet which lists out all the important things about your business. You want to document everything that you use and do in your business so that it's at least somewhere because if you're hospitalized or you can't work, there's something that someone could pick up from."

What goes into that book? Keldie says, "Think about tasks that you do in your business over and over and over again, the things that are recurring, so daily, weekly, monthly, quarterly, and annual taxes, and if you can even list those out without documenting them yet, at least what they are."

Starting with that list, you can flesh out your documentation further. Keldie says, "You can break that down even more to where you do a Loom video and a checklist with it because eventually you just use the checklist."

The checklist can be a valuable tool for outsourcing and also for yourself. Keldie shares, "Let's say you are in a lot of pain, you don't want to think anymore. So, what does the checklist say to do?" Having that checklist makes sure that you don't miss a step when you're not feeling well.

Checklists can also be helpful for prioritization. Keldie explains, "When you're managing your pain or an illness you might think, 'Okay, well I can do an hour's worth of work today. What are my priorities?' and you can look at what those tasks are that are set up for daily recurring and weekly recurring and figure out which ones are actually the tasks you need to do."

Documentation isn't static. It is a living, breathing guideline that will need ongoing maintenance. Keldie says, "Once you've got it done, then you can just keep updating it and reviewing it. If you're in doing something and the checklist is no longer relevant, then you need to update your process or rerecord the video if your strategy changes."

Sharon Benson talked about how she gets her clients to create documentation. "What I tell a lot of clients at first is to do a little video while you are doing whatever this task is, comment while you're going through it, and then take that video and give it to a virtual assistant to transcribe, to write it up, put it in the format of a Standard Operating Procedure (SOP)."

Once you have documentation it needs to be validated. Sharon recommends, "Have that new team member that's going to be doing that task, have them follow that SOP word for word, the client shouldn't say anything, but just watch." It's a matter of creating it, and then watching the person do it, and then refin[ing] it.

Documentation opens the door to confidence in outsourcing. When you have documentation, Sharon says, "it's got everything in it, then they can breathe and then they can delegate because they know that person has it, and they know if that person leaves, somebody else can pick it up, and go with it as well."

Sharon explains, "I think that's how you can make peace with it is just that trust factor. Knowing that it's been documented, anybody can pick it up and do it, and you can loosen the reins a little bit."

Cat Stancik agrees, explaining, "Delegating effectively all comes down to systems and documentation."

With that in mind, delegating effectively is what the next chapter is all about.

4
DELEGATE EFFECTIVELY

Chronic pain can be lonely but running your business doesn't have to be. Bringing in help can be so effective in reducing the number of hours you have to spend on your business, therefore increasing the number of hours you can spend taking care of yourself. You don't have to do it all alone. You just need to learn how to ask for help.

It sounds simple, but so often that's the hardest part. Teri Holland, Neuro-Linguistic Programming (NLP) trainer and business coach, talks about how delegating doesn't just help people who already have chronic pain. She says, "If you don't start delegating in your business, as an entrepreneur, and in systemizing things and getting all of that in place, then you might find that you end up with chronic pain from neglecting areas of your own health. Really, it's something that all entrepreneurs need to do. When you have chronic pain, you're forced to do it faster, I think. You don't get the choice; you have to do it."

Delegating can help you save money because as a business owner your time is valuable. You can save money by hiring somebody to do tasks that have a lower level of difficulty so that you can focus your efforts on higher return on investment (ROI) activities. Danielle Christopher, Vice President at Concito Design Group, came to realize this after she started delegating shop vac cleanup on job sites. That was a job she really didn't have to do.

Delegation can also help you save time. A task that isn't in your "zone of genius" (the thing you excel at) often can take longer for you to complete than somebody who is really good at it. You can save time by outsourcing a task to somebody who does it faster than you because it is his or her zone of genius. Tina Forsyth talks about a common trap people get themselves into when it comes to delegation. "It's always easiest at the moment to just do the thing — it will just take me a quick 15 minutes, no big deal." She cautions, "Well, let's add that up over time. Let's say in a given week, there are five different things that take 15 minutes each. That's 75 minutes a week, which adds up to 65 hours in a year. It always seems easier to do it in the moment but the reality is that every little thing adds up over time.

She recommends taking inventory of tasks like that. She says, "Make a list of everything you're doing every day for a week. Go back and look at that list. How many of those things were 'This is just a quick thing. I know I shouldn't be doing this, but I don't have anybody else.' How much of our week gets caught up in that stuff? You may be surprised to see."

Delegation can help you conserve energy. As a small-business owner, you might find that delegation isn't just something that needs to happen at the office. You can make a lot of gains in conserving energy by delegating tasks around the house and patching up day-to-day energy leaks at home.

Briar Harvey found that to be the case, relaying, "I have been married to a Marty Ginsburg for 20 years. At this point in time, I do not fold any laundry, I cook dinner two to three nights a week, and I don't clean. None of that would be possible if I didn't have a supportive partner, because he either does it, delegates it to the kids, or we figure out a way to pay for it."

Marketing Director Jenny Kanevsky found outsourcing household tasks were helpful for her, too, as she struggled with chronic pain. She shares, "I have a housekeeper, I don't clean my own house. It's a very worthwhile investment. I don't buy my own groceries, I have them delivered. Those are [the] kinds of things that are worth the investment for me, even though I might not be making tons and tons of money. The cost benefit of doing those things, versus me doing them for myself, and then exhausting myself and not having the energy to do what's really important [is worth it]."

That energy savings can make all the difference. More than saving it, redirecting it can also happen when you outsource or delegate tasks. You can start to focus on what lights you up.

Sharon Benson, certified Online Business Manager (OBM) trainer, says, "You really need to focus on figuring out what you do as a client, what your genius spot is." Narrowing down that list can happen by process of elimination. She suggests, "You can even make a yes and no list like, 'here's all the things I did this week. What are things that only I could do and what could I delegate to someone else that I don't have to do?'" She believes that, "once they have figured out what [only] they can do, everything else should be delegated."

Kim Strobel, Joy and Happiness Coach, agrees and she's really clear about what is in her zone of genius and what is not. "I'm not good at details, I can't handle details at all. I'm never going to be the person who wants to be in the weeds. I want to be out of the weeds."

She gets around those areas she doesn't enjoy by delegating. "I strategically hire people on my team who have a set of strengths that I'm missing, or that I'm completely uninterested in."

Her journey learning to delegate wasn't what she expected, but she learned how to do it well. She shares, "I actually think I'm really good at delegating. I was forced to, because my business grew really, really fast. I simply was suffocating, and I couldn't stay on top of it all."

As far as how much time she spends on tasks she enjoys and is good at, Kim says, "My goal is to be in my zone of genius 80 percent of the time, and then let my other team members who have a different skill set and are much better than me handle those pieces. I think that's the formula for success when you can do it."

Lana Welchman, NeuroKinetic Therapy (NKT) Exercise Therapist and pain-free fitness coach, takes a similar approach, explaining, "My plan is to outsource everything that isn't treating clients or working with clients which is why I got into this in the first place. I think it's just easy as an entrepreneur to feel overwhelmed by all the other things. What brings me joy is working with people and working with my clients. I am on the path to delegating everything else out."

Keldie Jamieson's approach to delegation is about alignment with interests and talent while considering fiscal realities. She counsels, "You do want to look at things that aren't in your zone of genius to hand off first, but it's also what you can afford. The reason that you want to start delegating is so that you have the energy left to do those things that only you can do that you're brilliant at."

Delegation is a great way to include more perspectives because the way you do things isn't the only way to do things. Tina shares her story of leaving room for more perspectives in her business. "When I hired my first Online Business Manager, Tiffany, years ago, one of the things she took over for me was communicating with clients. Sending welcome emails, reminders and such. I would read the email and my default response would be 'Oh, I wouldn't write it this way.'"

Letting go was a learning process for Tina and it helped to focus on the outcome rather than the process. "At first I would spend a bunch of time rewriting all of these emails she had sent to me for review. Then it occurred to me — are my edits necessary? Does her version serve the purpose and give the clients what they need to know? They feel welcomed. They've got the information they need. And even though it wasn't written exactly the way I would have written it, it still served the same function. And so I learned to let go and allow Tiffany to do it her way, even when it wasn't exactly the same as my way."

Also, if a task isn't in your zone of genius, it can be a way to improve quality by leaving it to the experts. Briar gives the following advice for finding your best fit for delegation, "It's finding someone who believes in the work that you're doing. If you can find someone who likes what you're doing, and who wants to help you succeed in that mission, then you can train them to do the work over time. And, in fact, they'll probably do it better than you. Because the things that we are hiring someone to replace us for are the things that we suck at anyway."

Delegation is the path to working on your business instead of in it. Keldie has inspiring words for those looking to step into their role as CEO of their business through delegation. "Let's think bigger. So, you're the CEO of Coca-Cola. Do you actually know how to do the packaging? Do you actually know how to clean the bottles or set up the canning machine or different things like that? You don't. You learn to delegate."

But first, you have to be able to ask for help.

Making Peace with Asking for Help

Asking for help can make you feel incredibly vulnerable. Lots of people struggle with it and there is temptation to soldier on because of the entrepreneurial culture around hustle that you just need to work harder and longer and grind it out. This can be really unhelpful for people struggling with chronic pain.

Ultimately, there's no shame in asking for help. Hilary Jastram shares her story of making peace with asking for help: "The only way to trust is to trust. That is exactly what I had to do. I had to jump in and hell or high water, no matter what came up or from it."

Asking for help and letting go wasn't always easy for Hilary. In her experience, "the hardest thing was doing less, it was doing less and watching other people do things, the way I would not do them, and communicate in the way I would not communicate."

Letting go can be hard when ego gets in the way. Hilary struggled with that, explaining "I always thought that what I did was best, it got results. Because I was like a little badger with a sledgehammer trying to get responses from people, but it always worked. I was very persistent."

There came a point where she had to start letting other people do things. "When I got sick, I was like, "Well, the dishes aren't going to be done my way, the laundry is not going to be done my way. The rearing of the children isn't going to be done my way' ... I had to let all of it go," Hilary remembers.

It came down to priorities and prioritizing her wellness. She realized, "It doesn't matter how the dishes are done. It doesn't matter how the kids are picked up. It doesn't matter how the bills are paid; it doesn't matter. None of it matters. It is so small. Letting go of those smaller pieces was the greatest release I have ever felt in my life. I try not to forget that as I try to get better. I try not to lose that that was a critical watershed moment."

She also learned to reframe asking for help as a way of helping others. "You're helping with the abundance in somebody else's life and you get to feel good about that, even though it feels kind of selfish," she suggested.

Danielle Christopher struggled with letting go and asking for help too. In her case, she said, "It was so hard. But I finally had to go, "In order for me to get better, now I'm going to have to outsource." She found comfort in being able to help people earn a living through her outsourcing.

"It felt better during [the pandemic] because we were keeping people employed. That actually felt good as a business owner going, 'OK, that person didn't have to go on CERB [Canadian government pandemic assistance] because they were able to work for us.' We took a bit of a financial hit, but it also meant we were keeping some local dads employed."

Asking for help and what it meant doing so was initially a stumbling block for Danielle. "I was giving myself permission to accept that I'm not Superwoman. It was hard at first to admit defeat, I felt defeated. I felt horrible. I felt less than. I thought, 'That's it, my husband's going to want me to be out of the business.'"

Ultimately, Danielle was able to focus on her recovery to get over it and find peace and better take care of herself by delegating things in her business.

Lana Welchman struggled with control too and had to learn to let go. She got through it by getting real about her values, explaining, "I have to ask myself, what is more important, my time and my sanity? And not sitting in front of a computer for hours? Yes. Or that little bit of control?"

Briar Harvey saw the value of delegating and if she were to change anything in her business as an entrepreneur struggling with chronic pain, she says, "I would have hired much, much sooner. Because having support for the things that you don't want to do makes a huge difference."

When it comes time to delegate, lots of business owners worry about making their first hire. They share fears such as "What if they suck? What if I hire the wrong person?" Tina Forsyth's advice is simple, "I lovingly call myself and most of my clients a recovering control freak. As a default, I'm going to do it myself. I know I do it the best. But that's this dangerous trap to be in. As long as we operate from that place, everything is going to continue to be on our plates."

That fear can keep people from making the leap, but it doesn't have to. Tina says, "When people ask, 'How do I know if I can find the right person?' I equate it to dating. When we are interested in marriage, we will generally date a number of people before we find the right one."

"Yes, there is a strategy to hiring that we want to learn. But we also want to allow ourselves to take the risk of making a 'bad hire.' Even if we don't find the right person the first time around, we learn and try again."

You can mitigate risk that comes with a new hire by being strategic about where you position your team member, she suggests. "When someone is new to the team don't put them in a client-facing position right away. Don't have them doing work that is essential to the business. If the person is not a good fit and does a poor job that can be tougher to recover from. Start them simple, and work with them to learn the business and as they prove themselves in the role have them step up in bigger ways."

You also need to let go of the fear your new hire will make a mistake. Tina says, "They most likely will make a mistake! The fact they made the mistake isn't the issue as we are all imperfect, what I'm more concerned with is how do they respond. Do they take ownership of the mistake and fix it? Let them make the mistake. Let them fix it."

You also need to let go of the fear your new hire will make a mistake. Tina says, "What if they make a mistake? That probably will happen, I can pretty much guarantee it. Let them make the mistake. Let them fix it."

It's a risk, but it's worth it. Teri Holland talks about how she decided it was time to ask for help. She says, "I looked at, 'What is it costing me to not ask for help? What's the cost of not asking for help?' and usually entrepreneurs don't like things that cost. What is it costing you to stay this way and not ask for help?" If we're really honest with ourselves, we can see the truth of what not asking for help is doing for our bodies and our businesses.

Delegating can be such a powerful way of taking care of yourself for entrepreneurs. It takes a village to raise a child and it takes a team to build a business when you need to prioritize taking care of yourself. In these cases, asking for help is a sign of strength, not weakness. It's a commitment to growth and it's a commitment to yourself.

Asking for help is a form of self-care, but it's not always easy to do. A lot of it has to do with the things that we believe about work, making money, and what it means about us. Tina explains, "We feel like we have to be working hard to be worthy."

Tim Salau sees asking for help as balance and modernizing your company. "We have to stop glorifying that work is the be all end all when it comes to careers. I'm grateful that Guide is an early stage of growth, that we're able to design our culture from the ground up, even as we scale it's going to be the same way because we're a remote-first company."

As a thought leader in the area of work, he sees what happens to businesses that haven't evolved, explaining, "most organizations are still really operating under traditional constructs of what makes a successful working culture, what makes a successful organization, a lot of organizations are still, fundamentally, doing business with ideologies from the 1990s or the 1980s, which is to compete, compete, compete, compete, compete." He believes there's a better way.

The truth is, asking for help is necessary for growth.

Keldie Jamieson opines, "You can't scale a business without delegating and bringing team members on eventually. At some point, we all have to delegate to someone."

Tina shares the same opinion, explaining, "The only way to get ourselves out of being the hub and being the center of the business is to have a team in place. Because without that, there's really no way to get ourselves out of the whole thing."

When budgets are tight, delegating can feel overwhelming, but Tina recommends a mindset shift when evaluating if it's time to delegate. "If we look through the lens of what it's going to cost us then we may never want to spend money on a team. But if we look through the lens of how valuable our own time is — and own the fact that when we are caught in the 'little things' it's actually keeping us away from growing our own business. If you're so busy over here in the weeds, that you don't have time to go and sell something, then that's the cycle that needs to be broken. Hiring someone to get you out of the weeds so you can grow the business — that is what breaks the cycle."

Tim has advice on getting around the costs of delegation by thinking globally. He says, "You have optionality in how you design your workforce and build your culture and hire talent. The advantage of the future of work in the global economy that we're now living in is that you can find talented people anywhere, and you can pay them fair market value based on where they live, or what their asking price is. That's optionality, and that optionality is really powerful for any organization. This optionality and expansion of the gig economy but also the world of global and remote work, it allows any organization to play beyond their strengths."

Melissa Rodgers offers a cautionary note around outsourcing that is worth considering. She says, "I think a lot of people kind of close their eyes and take the leap when it comes to outsourcing. They don't look at it from a numbers perspective. It's not always the right move to outsource the thing you don't like doing."

She suggests being strategic about what you outsource, explaining, "A lot of people don't want to hear that because we wish that we could outsource everything that we don't like doing but often that is not a money making activity, and it's not necessarily integral to your bottom line. Investing in it, just because you don't like it and then continuing to scramble and not be able to meet your deliverables for everything else that is money making is just going to leave you in the hole."

Melissa takes a tough love approach in holding herself accountable. "You have to be really brutal with yourself and say like, 'I don't really like this task. But what is the task that if I outsource it, I'm going to get more than what I've spent back in ROI?'

Whatever you decide to outsource, you need to figure out how to ask for help.

Ultimately, you need to get out of your own way if you want to succeed, and you need to be willing to bring in more people if you get stuck, or to prevent getting stuck altogether. The world is your oyster, and there are so many opportunities to bring brilliant people into your business.

It would be nice to think that we can delegate every unpleasant task but being strategic with your delegation is what is going to best position you to move forward with confidence.

How to Ask for Help

Asking for help can be hard not just from an ego perspective, but also literally, and knowing how to ask for help can assist you in acquiring the best result for your company. A lot of it has to do with our attitudes about delegation. Tina Forsyth says, "We think delegation should be easy but the truth is it's not ... especially in the beginning. When we can accept that it's tough and may feel uncomfortable at first, then we are much more likely to stick with it and that's when it will really pay off down the road."

Using SMART principles (specific, measurable, achievable, realistic, and time bound) can be helpful in accurately describing a task, but it's also about asking the right person, Teri Holland explains.

"I won't ask for help from just anybody, but finding someone who's really skilled in what they do and someone I really trust is important to me. I think sometimes we think we have to trust everyone or be vulnerable with everyone and you don't, you can be very selective with who you ask for help from and make sure that that person is someone who's in alignment with your values."

You need to do your homework about who you are bringing into your business and that means consulting online reviews, picking up the phone, scheduling interviews and discovery calls, and discerning who is going to be the best fit for you. Spend some time putting into words exactly what you need, and be really specific in breaking down the tasks so you can establish scope.

5

PERSPECTIVE SHIFT:
REFRAME YOUR STORY

Entrepreneurs dealing with chronic pain know what a limit feels like. It can be vulnerable to admit that there is a limit to what you can do, and you can carry a lot of shame around that.

You can choose to think about it differently though. Your limit could be your secret weapon. It's all a matter of perspective.

What's getting in the way could be the way you connect with your people. By identifying your "weaknesses," repositioning them as an advantage, and owning your reality without apology, you can see your limits differently (reframe them in your mind), and reshape how people see you.

The way you tell your story can build trust with your audience. It explains your worldview and helps them get to know the person they are going to be working with. It can set you apart from the crowd, it can show your resilience, and it can create the mental image of you as a conqueror instead of a victim.

Melissa Rodgers has experienced that herself and shares, "I think the reality is that if you are going through something, other people are going through it. There are ways to weave your story and your struggles into your brand without that being your whole identity. I want to lead with what I can offer, and what results I can create and transformation so I can offer for other people. And then once in a while I will weave in some of my personal story."

That selective vulnerability can make a big impact. Melissa shared a story of what happened when she shared her personal life. "Someone sent me a message the other day. She said, 'Even though you don't talk about it, very much there's palpable authenticity to your brand,' and that was her wording."

Melissa thinks it's all in how you talk about what you're going through and, "I think that is what happens when you're honest about what it is that you're going through without offering it up as an excuse or as the only thing about you. Especially if you're dealing with a health issue or chronic pain like it, there's no getting away from it. It's part of you, it's part of your daily life."

Letting people into your world can help you build relationships, she explains. "To try and hide it or try to push it aside is not going to be beneficial to you mentally, but it's also shutting your followers out, it's shutting your potential buyers out of a really key part of your life that allows all the pieces of you to click into place for them."

Melissa explains it as a way to humanize yourself to your customers, "When they have that whole picture, and that's not to say that you share all of your private life, I'm still a real person. I'm not a robotic business service, you put coins in, and you get marketing out, that's not how it works. That affords me grace when I need it."

Nicole Kaufman, a North Carolina-based therapist who works with high-performing female entrepreneurs, offers this advice: "This adventure of entrepreneurship is fun, because it comes through you. Our business is not a thing you do, or a thing that happens with only your help. Your business happens through you being able to bring your unique flavor to the population you serve. Chronic pain or not, your story is your story. Nobody can really do that like you can."

She encourages clients to keep that in mind when they are thinking about their limitations and says, "your mindset around the competing ideas of 'Do I deserve to be here? I can't work a full 40-hour week or I'm in pain half the time. Do I even deserve to be doing this? Who will listen to what I have to say? When that imposter syndrome comes up around this, we have to remember, it's your flavor that is coming through. You may not have any ground-breaking research or world-altering thoughts, and that's okay. Spirit has moved you to be in the place that you are, to have these thoughts ... and they are going to change someone's life because you said them or wrote them. And that, my dear, is enough."

Chronic pain is not your whole identity, but it can help people understand who you are and where you're coming from. Chronic pain is really common, and many people will be able to relate to your story.

How to Mitigate a "Disadvantage"

Chronic pain can feel like a real disadvantage, but Cat offers a different way of looking at the way we see weakness. She says, "We've been socialized into believing that we need to have this holistic, well-rounded personality that conforms to a lot of expectations. I think that when you look at successful entrepreneurs, and you look at successful people, what they've actually done is gone left when everybody's been telling them to go right. What I mean by that is that instead of trying to improve their weaknesses, what they've done is actually reinforced their strengths, really leaning into what is it that makes them unique."

She talks about "weakness" in terms of being a way to differentiate yourself, even with clients who don't struggle with chronic pain. "I talk sometimes about the things that made you weird and awkward and socially inept in high school and in grade school are actually the things that make you attractive and desirable by people out there. When you are able to demonstrate success, and demonstrate personality, it gives other people that permission to be able to do the same."

Rachel Barbic, business strategist, believes in finding your own way, weakness or not. She says, "The only way to have sustainable success is to find the right things that fit for you and can be worked around and the limitations you have. I think we all want to be able to do more than we can. We think we can, and we assume we can, and we put pressure on ourselves instead of trying to create things that work for us. We are all individual, unique people and our needs, no matter what limitations we have, are just as unique. And our business can't be forced into a blueprint that someone else created for them."

Tim has dealt with perceived weakness in a different context than chronic pain, but the lessons are very much applicable to the pain experience. He says, "I'm a Black founder. I'm underrepresented because of the color of my skin. I'm not traditional. Fortunately, I'm wealthy and built my wealth through hard work and grit. I have a huge personal brand. I have all of these things going for me, but I'm still faced with this narrative of less than 1 percent of Black founders getting venture capital. That's not the narrative I choose to claim though. It's not even my narrative, but I can empathize with underrepresented founders that no one believes in or no one will give an opportunity to. I grew up in the hood, the streets, I know what underrepresented looks like. I used to live in filth. Thankfully, I don't live in filth anymore, but I didn't achieve the accolades and where I am at by sitting on my butt. I worked. And I surrounded myself with the right people."

He sees that "weakness" and unlikelihood in a different light, explaining, "That's the narrative that often people try to drive deep into people who are nontraditional, people who are unconventional, people who come from an outsider's perspective. It's like, 'You can't do this because you're just this, or you're part of this Indigenous tribe or you're Black or you're too creative.'"

He rejects this as being a true disadvantage and instead offers, "The reality is that actually, no, we don't even need your capital because ownership of my company is better and more importantly, you can build an amazing company without diluting your company. A lot of entrepreneurs fall for bad narratives that actually don't reflect their ability to build an amazing business or live an amazing life through their business."

The truth is the things that bring us to our knees are so often the things that make us stronger. When you don't have as much time, energy, or capital to work with, you have to get creative and find unconventional solutions.

Your ability to problem-solve around your condition is something you can use in your client work to stand out. You have a unique perspective as someone navigating pain and you can use that way of seeing things to find a way through for the people you support.

When you can't do things the way everyone else does, you can often find a better way of doing things. You look for the shortcuts out of necessity where others aren't as likely to challenge themselves to find new solutions. You have a bigger reason to find the best way: so you can survive and thrive.

Find the Right Market for You

Sometimes instead of mitigating a perceived disadvantage, the best course of action is to find a market that doesn't see it as one. Melissa Rodgers shared her story of finding a market that doesn't care.

"I had to become self-employed when I had my first baby and I became the caregiver for my siblings. I was working in project management at the time, which is not family friendly, they could not offer me any flexibility. I had to figure out how to replace my salary. But I also couldn't go to the Chamber of Commerce meeting, and I couldn't go rub shoulders with all of these businesspeople that I knew had the money to invest in my services."

So, she took a different path.

"I started building my web design business. At the time, I noticed that the clients that I had the most fun working with and felt the least stress working with and the clients that were the least stressed working with me were other moms."

Finding your niche can make all the difference in terms of identifying a market that doesn't care about your perceived disadvantage. Selecting the wrong niche can be problematic. "There are certain niches that require you to be on all the time, and require you to be very present, they require a lot of travel and things that you just can't offer as a parent typically of young children or as someone with really any mitigating circumstance."

Finding a market that doesn't care about Melissa's schedule was key to her finding balance as a new mom.

"Whether it's a health issue, a family issue, the early years of my business were some of the most tumultuous in my life to date, and things were crazy. There were definitely times when I completely dropped the ball, because things were so bad. The majority of the experience was that I was able to push through and my clients were able to give me grace, and I was able to give them grace."

Ultimately that grace being a two-way street is crucial. Melissa shared, "I remember one of my first branding clients was a newly single mom, she was just dealing with the upheaval of divorce, and she had a really hard time getting back to me on time, she was really having a hard time essentially fulfilling her obligations as a client. I will never forget working with her because she was so grateful that

I was flexible with her, and I didn't charge her additional fees and things like that. It was that mutual understanding. There's that mutual respect for the fact that life happens."

Find a Process That Doesn't Need What You Don't Have

One of the joys of entrepreneurship is that you can design or "reframe" your processes around your limitations.

Dana Corey, business coach, did just that. "I only work with my clients on the phone, even before this pandemic. Part of what drove me to that is that it gives me control over what position my body can be in."

Jake Schaap gives this advice to his chronically ill clients to imagine what is possible instead of focusing on what is not: "Look at yourself, objectively take a step back and just think for a second, 'What is the best way that I can optimize? What I can control? And what are the things I can't control? What are the obtainable goals? What are the stretch goals? What are the things that I can really knock out while I'm sitting in bed?'"

For Hilary Jastram, the key to a sustainable process is planning ahead. "You plan for those days. That's why you build in a two-day cushion for your deadline. It's why you do different things because you know, you're going to feel like crap. So how are you going to manage when you feel like crap so that the whole thing doesn't go up in flames?"

Dusti Arab agrees with the value of planning ahead. "I think that one of the hardest things for new entrepreneurs is showing up consistently. If you're in pain on a schedule that you can't predict, you need to try and build in as much flexibility as possible into your work. Try to build in flexibility so that you can show up for your clients when you're able to show up for your clients."

Melissa Rodgers believes in planning ahead through leveraging time well to create resources for sick time. "It's really nice if you can take the time when you are feeling well, when you're feeling balanced, and there isn't a lot of stress going on, if you can take the time to create resources for yourself that you can utilize repeatedly. You're essentially systematizing your workflow for delivery of your offer."

It's about not being in denial. Hilary advocates for acceptance, "You have to accept the fact, I'm going to feel like crap. I'm going to do the best I can to manage it and I'm going to try and bring the flames down as much as possible so they're not engulfing me so I can do some work. But on days when I do feel like crap, it's OK."

The other piece is setting yourself up for success instead of fighting your limitations.

Keldie Jamieson recommends that "If your brain is on fire in the morning, and that's when you do your best writing and you need to write, then you need to prioritize it for the morning. It's about knowing what you can cope with."

Personally, my hands swell when I type. That's why I create content from transcripts. I dictate copy, which is perfect because the best copy is conversational. I dictate everything I can, and that's how I have come to be a writer who doesn't type.

It's All in How You Choose to Do It

You can make a disadvantage an advantage by finding a market that celebrates the way you work and reframing the way you talk about your challenges. When I was first starting out, I would hear from other virtual assistants that they couldn't charge as much money because they were only available evenings and weekends because they had day jobs.

I always challenged them to reposition their services as support available in the evenings and weekends exclusively and that they specialize in supporting entrepreneurs who like to work those hours. That's a service not available from every service provider and while it might feel like a disadvantage to have limited hours, it could actually be an advantage. It all depends who you're selling to.

As someone with chronic pain, you would do well to position yourself as an innovator. When dealing with chronic pain, there's so much need for innovation and finding new solutions and work-arounds to deal with challenges as they come up. That makes those of us with chronic pain naturally great problem solvers and an asset to any client.

Ultimately, it comes down to being real and being honest about who you are and what you're about. Hilary Jastram says, "That's the anti-hustle and what I like to call the sick hustle. This is real. Work is done sometimes in pajama pants, sometimes it's done in bed, but [you] have to break that stigma and be that rabid cheerleader for yourself."

6
REFUEL:
SELF-CARE FOR CHRONIC PAIN

As they say, you can't pour from an empty cup. To truly thrive you need to take care of yourself. Self-care matters for chronic pain.

Too often, not taking care of ourselves can lead to more problems. Those of us dealing with chronic pain have a higher need for self-care; the care that allows us to do what we do day in and day out.

That was certainly Jake Schaap's experience. He says, "I had the colitis, chronic pain constantly and to be honest, I didn't really eat well, I was over-stressing myself, I was really doing everything that you shouldn't do. When you're sick, when you have an autoimmune disease, when you have a chronic illness, you shouldn't do the things I did. Stress typically brings on the symptoms and the flare-ups of chronic illness a lot of times."

Jenny Kanevsky's advice from her years of experience with chronic pain is to be intentional about self-care, working it into your schedule to make sure that it happens. She sees self-care as being a mix of exercise, healthy eating, and adequate rest.

Amber Ingraham speaks to the consequences of not performing appropriate self-care, noting that without it, pain can worsen. She reinforces that you need to build a business that works for you, instead of trying to fit yourself into a business model that doesn't.

Stress can significantly impact your ability to be creative. One of my clients, Gail Johnson, a midwife, explains how stress stops labor in animals and prevents them from being able to progress. I often use that as an example when I'm explaining to people the impact of stress on creativity. You can't deliver an idea under stress; like an animal's labor, it is impeded by that stress. That mindset is not ideal for creating or problem-solving. We don't deliver our best solutions under pressure. Taking care of yourself is a good way to manage stress.

Self-care Is More Than Bubble Baths

The commercialization of self-care has led to assumptions about what it involves and how to effectively care for your body. That constant messaging around spas and relaxation really limits the imagination on what we can do to help ourselves.

Jen Campbell, cofounder of Balance365, challenges her clients to redefine self-care. She says, "We know that there's an industry that has risen up around self-care that is often just pushing consumer consumption, it's pushing consumption as self-care."

She offers a different perspective on self-care. "That's not what I would define as self-care, I would define self-care as looking at your different facets of wellness, which would be your physical, emotional, spiritual. And then, of course, there's the 'get stuff done' self-care: booking your appointments, getting your groceries, that kind of thing, the self-care it requires to function and cope as a basic human being who has to eat, sleep, go to the bathroom and just function."

Jake Schaap, similarly, offers a different perspective on self-care that exists outside the realm of bubble baths. He recommends, "Figure out how much sleep you actually need; everyone operates differently. Figure out your specific diet, and even write down what times of days you're eating. Just figure out a routine for yourself and what really works."

It isn't a quick fix, he explains, "Unfortunately, what people don't like to hear is, this takes time to figure it out. Because you have to listen to your body and even your body is going to be out of whack sometimes, but you need to figure out how your body is operating, what your routines and schedules are going to be and then from there, you can look at: 'What work can I do? What best fits into my routine and lifestyle from there?' But it takes time."

Self-care can be as practical and simple as something such as ergonomics. Lana Welchman had to re-evaluate her self-care at a certain point. "When the pandemic hit, I started working at my kitchen table. It was horrible. My first advice is to make sure that you have a set-up, wherever you are working, that works for your body. Something that's ergonomically sound, and that you can adjust." She advocates for healthy working conditions because as a wellness professional who works with injured people, she sees the damage it can do. "My first advice to people is set your space up so you can work without causing a ton more pain. My second advice would be to not just set up your workstation, like your desk, but set up a space where you can take breaks and be able to manage your pain however you manage it for yourself."

What that space looks like will vary from person to person, she acknowledges, "There are a million ways to manage your pain — medication, mindset, meditation, and exercise — all sorts of things. Allow yourself the physical space to do that. Set up a little area in your office and allow yourself a mental space to do that as well because I feel like especially when you are dealing with chronic pain, it is so easy to fall into kind of this pain spiral where you just kind of [let it] drag you down. Allow yourself the space both physically and mentally to manage your pain and tell yourself it's OK to do that."

Lana reinforces the need for self-care particularly for entrepreneurs with chronic pain, counseling, "your body, your well-being comes first. You can't run a successful business and you can't put the focus you need into it if you are constantly getting dragged down by your pain."

Therapist Nicole Kaufman asks her clients, "Are you serving your business and serving yourself? How are you dealing with your medical condition, as well as everything else?" She wants them to understand that "The business will still be there, but it's not going to be there if you're not. Get your head off the computer, relax, do what you need to do, go to your appointments, take your meds as directed. Do what's being asked of you to do. Because we want you around."

Self-care As Boundaries

Beyond bubble baths and setting up your physical space for success, self-care can look like boundaries. Kim Strobel shares from her experience coaching women, explaining, "As women, we are inherently people pleasers. We've come from generations of women who have told us that everybody else counts before us. If there's anything left over at the end of the day, then you can have some. But guess what? There's nothing ever left if we followed this formula."

More than not taking time for ourselves, Kim talks about how too often we don't honor our own desires. She says, "Women consistently say yes to shit we don't want to do and we do it all the time. That leaves us feeling angry, resentful, and pissed off a lot of the time. What I really want women to know is that when you are a 'yes' to shit you don't want to do you're also a 'no' to stuff you really do want to do. You really have to decide which feels better."

She acknowledges setting boundaries is not necessarily easy, and that there may be consequences. "Sometimes along this journey, you will experience the fallout of some of your interpersonal relationships. You've inadvertently trained people that you show up and always do what's best for everyone else. And when you decide to change, there may be some pushback. But that is really where you stand in your power and you find your strength."

Does that mean Kim never does anything she doesn't want to do? "Of course, I still say yes to some stuff I don't want to do because I'm a good person. Sometimes we do have to put ourselves out for others. But I have learned to say no to a lot of stuff so that I can say yes to things that I have decided are more important in my life and better for me."

Sheila Sutherland speaks to how she uses boundaries for self-care, explaining, "I have to listen to my body. I spent decades not listening to my body and pushing through, and just doing what I thought needed to be done. I can't do that anymore. I'm having to redesign a different life. And I'm still in the process of figuring what that looks like."

Sometimes the boundaries we need to create aren't with people but with ourselves and with our activities.

Jen Campbell speaks to this from her experience coaching women in Balance365, sharing, "There are boundaries, I think, that a lot of entrepreneurs have to create with technology, even though they live in a technology world. We still need boundaries around technology. I bring up technology because people think it's one of the biggest unacknowledged distractions in our world. Our brains were not designed to live in such a distracting world."

Jen creates boundaries around technology so that she can be more successful and at peace, explaining, "I have no alerts on my phone, the only thing I have that goes off on my phone is my alarm in the morning. I get a buzzer at night when it's time to power down."

Further, she asserts, "Sleep is like a reset for the human body, hormonally, psychologically, physically. I think sleep is probably the number one thing that entrepreneurs need to have boundaries around. For me, it's just getting very honest about how creative I'm able to be when I'm very tired. When you're very tired, you're just working the motions, you're just walking through life as a zombie. My business requires me to be creative, every single day."

Taking care of herself with sleep allows Jen to take care of her clients better, she explains, "My business still requires a lot of time, attention, creativity, and because I run a coaching business, [it requires me] holding space for other people a lot and as an entrepreneur who has a team, holding space for my team. There's just so much that has to go into protecting my brain. I would say sleep is probably the number one thing that I can do to protect my brain."

Sherry Edmunds-Flett, Executive Director of LINC, an organization that supports community reintegration for people in conflict with the law, and victim-offender reconciliation, struggles with chronic pain and has had to institute boundaries as self-care. She said, "I can't do all that I used to do when I was able-bodied. What I have to do now is I have to really pick what I want to focus on, I have to be really clear about my focus, because I can't be all things to all people."

Meagan Hamilton, a therapist known as The Assertive Mama who has a course on boundaries, shares, "My biggest philosophy is that it is OK to say 'no, I don't want to do this. I can't meet you. No, I'm struggling this month. I can't take on that project.' It's practicing doing a little bit less. And ultimately, it's saying 'no,' or sharing, 'I can't support that right now. But let's assess that next month.'"

Beyond the intrapersonal conflict that can result in setting certain boundaries, Meagan helps people deal with the internal conflicts that can result from saying no to something. "The consequence of saying no is that guilt that we feel. So, I have a conversation with a lot of people that say that to me, and I ask, 'Well, what are you actually doing wrong?'"

Her perspective on guilt has a positive spin. "Guilt is an important emotion. Guilt gets a bad rap and is there to alert us that something we're doing isn't right. We're really perceiving guilt; it's not actually real guilt. And if we say yes to everything, we're actually saying no to ourselves."

It's also about the delivery of the no. We can mitigate a lot of conflict when we say no by choosing the words that we use carefully. "If we say no to things more often, and it doesn't need to be a harsh 'no,' it can be, 'Not right now. Let me think about it. How about you ask me again next month ... next week?' Those are ways of negotiating a bit of time and space, which may feel a little less harsh. That's generally when I start working with people around boundaries and assertiveness. It's not this hammer crushing 'no', it's learning to be a little bit uncomfortable and that negotiation piece, certainly."

The timing of saying no is important. Meagan shares, "People generally do not start being assertive and creating healthy boundaries for themselves until they are worn out, injured, ill, suffer an extreme health challenge, and realize 'I can't keep operating the same way.' So, the unfortunate part about us as humans is we generally wait until there's a catastrophic problem."

When their clients are looking for places to start introducing boundaries, Teri Holland suggests, "The first thing is understanding your values, because our boundaries are created by our values. The first step is understanding what's the most important to me, what's most important to me, in my health, in my relationships, in my business, in my overall life, what are my values?"

That understanding can give us contacts when we start experiencing difficult emotions around boundaries. Teri explains, "When we have feelings, like anger, [that] is a warning that someone or something is pushing up on your values, then you need to know that's a good indication that your boundaries are being pressed. If you feel guilt, it's when we press up against our own values, our own boundaries."

Her advice to clients who are struggling with guilt is, "When it comes to saying no, I think it's only uncomfortable the first time. It's like the first time you ask for your new rate in business, it's awkward the first time but then it's over and you did it. The world doesn't end. Nothing bad happens. And you realize that you can say no to more things."

There is something to be said for boundaries and self-care. Warren Buffett was quoted as saying that "Really successful people say no to almost everything." Life coach Susan Hyatt encourages her clients to consider self-care as a business plan. Business coach Rachel Rodgers has encouraged her clients to take care of themselves because how they feel is one of the biggest predictors of how successful they can be and how productive they can be.

Self-care is the number one way you can build resilience against the ups and downs of business. What that looks like is personal to you, but it's important to figure out.

7

GIVE YOURSELF A BREAK: SELF-COMPASSION FOR SUCCESS

As business owners, we always need to innovate, and in order to innovate we need to be able to practice self-compassion.

If you want to create solutions, you need to get comfortable with forgiving yourself when things don't work out as planned. Innovation requires you to get back up when you fail, and keep trying.

Pace Yourself

Therapist Nicole Kaufman tells her clients that it's a marathon, not a sprint. It's about not getting ahead of yourself, not comparing yourself to where you think you should be. This is especially true for chronic pain people, because you are going to work differently than someone who is not dealing with chronic pain. You may work different hours; you may have to sub out more and that's OK. The only one who really cares if you overwork yourself is you. Have you gotten sick of your body screaming at you for doing this? If so, talk to someone about how to take the little things off your to-do list. Even hiring a house cleaner once a month can be life-changing.

Be Realistic

Nicole Kaufman advocates for self-compassion on the basis that we hold ourselves to unrealistic standards. "There's not one way to be an entrepreneur, to run one's business. As entrepreneurs, we get caught up in what we see on the internet, what we see other people doing, 'I should be there,' that whole destination addiction thing, 'I should be so much further ahead,' or 'I'll be happy when', or even 'I'll be in less pain when this gets done, or I reach this milestone, or this happens.'" Putting off our happiness into some future that hasn't happened yet prevents us from enjoying the present moment.

She continues, "You might only work two hours a day, because that's what you can do that day. If the pain is too much, honor it, don't fight it. Give yourself the grace and compassion to work your business the way that you need to work it in order that you are taken care of. All entrepreneurs are trying for life-balance, you just happen to be juggling the extra ball labeled "chronic pain."

Practice Gratitude

Kim Strobel approaches self-compassion as an extension of self-love, explaining, "I try to make at least one or two of my daily gratitudes a self-love gratitude for myself. We also don't take the time to acknowledge the good things that we're doing and that's a self-love issue. I want to extend that kindness back on myself as well."

Banish Your Inner Critic

Kim Strobel acknowledges, "We are hardest on ourselves. We very easily get the good old ball and chain out and whip ourselves across the back for all of the ways in which we are inadequate, and not enough. We have that inner critic voice in the back of our heads that is constantly talking to us and telling us that."

This was becoming a problem for Kim who explained, "I have had trouble extending grace, and compassion to myself, I can give it to every other human being, but I have found it difficult to give to myself. Recently, when I was in therapy, my therapist was trying to teach me how to extend some loving kindness to myself, and I literally could not do it. I teach all this about self-love. I feel like I love myself a lot more than I used to. But I couldn't say it because it didn't feel like the truth to me."

Kim found a solution in therapy, deciding to channel the kindness of her friend to override her inner critic and learn to love herself the way others love her.

Stop Fearing Failure

Jake Schaap suggests that you need to "be very forgiving of yourself when you're trying to figure this out because you are going to mess up a lot. But you're going to find out a lot about yourself as well and you're going to understand more of your capacity as a chronically ill individual. Don't be scared to mess up. Because you will, failure is inevitable, especially when you're getting into something new."

Manage Emotional Pain to Reduce Physical Pain

Sheila Sutherland sees the connection between the lack of self-compassion and an increase in pain. "If I emotionally get wound up about not being able to do something, that emotional trigger will trigger more pain. Some of it is around managing expectations and that we don't need to beat ourselves up quite so badly. One step forward, even if it's a tiny little baby step, is still moving forward."

By pacing yourself, being realistic, practicing gratitude, banishing your inner critic, destigmatizing failure, and getting a handle on your feelings, you can use self-compassion to propel you forward. Beating yourself up robs you of the momentum you need to move forward. When your energy is limited, it's counterproductive to expend it on self-flagellation.

8

COPE WITH BIG PROBLEMS AND BIG FEELINGS

One of the most frustrating things about chronic pain is that so often people will say it's all in your head. I'm here to tell you that your pain is real, but the answer to dealing with the big feelings that come from chronic pain could be in your head.

Mindfulness and meditation can be powerful tools for increasing your resilience, managing the emotions that come with pain, and being more present in your life. As chronic pain patients, there is a tendency to dissociate because reality is too uncomfortable. Showing up more can actually make things better. Meditation can help get you there more comfortably.

How Meditation Can Help Manage Chronic Pain

Therapist Nicole Kaufman says, "If you don't have a meditation, a guided meditation, or a decent meditation practice going for yourself that you do at least once a day, for 20 to 30 minutes, you're missing out on the opportunity to really take your business to the next level."

It doesn't just help with your business; it can also help with your pain. Chronic pain can be a challenge that comes with big feelings. Learning how to cope is key.

Mindfulness can be really helpful for chronic pain, as Sheila Sutherland discovered. "The biggest thing that helped with my pain was meditation. I have not kept up my practice as regularly as I need to, but when I allow my mind and body to have that, even if it's just a half hour, just to sit in silence. It does a lot for me."

But how do you know that it's time to explore mindfulness and meditation? Meditation teacher Wendy Kapty-Weymann says you can tell in a few ways, including, "definitely the obsessive thinking and the constant worrying about it. If it's really weighing on you, or you find yourself in a loop, thinking about it with circular thinking, like that hamster wheel or if you find it's really preoccupying you."

It's important to be honest with yourself when you're assessing if mindfulness is something that could be helpful for you. Wendy says, "I encourage people even just to kind of start to notice, 'how often are you thinking about this?' They don't even realize and then it's like, 'oh my gosh, I think about this every ten minutes. I'm spending hours thinking about this during the day.'"

There are other signs that it might be time to slow down and be mindful. Wendy recommends considering meditation, "If you find you're experiencing anxiety, or panic attacks about it. Meditation is proven to drastically reduce anxiety."

It isn't just research that tells her that. She's seen it firsthand, "I've personally experienced that. I've had lots of clients with chronic pain, they just start to sink into a depression, and it can be hard to pull yourself out of that. That's another signal that meditation might be really helpful. The other nice thing about meditation when you're depressed is that sometimes it's like when you're depressed, going to yoga class or doing movement can be too much. With meditation, all you have to do is sit there."

Wendy is a meditation teacher who has personal experience with pain. She says, "I've personally dealt with chronic pain. I find my meditation practices help so much. The thing is, with chronic pain, there's the actual pain, but then there's all of the stories that we're creating around it, and then all the additional suffering that we're creating around it in our minds."

She knows what that's like, explaining, "I had a neck injury for years, and my neck was sore, but then I would go to these places of like, 'Oh my god, I'm never going to be able to sit and read a book; oh, my God, I'm going to be in pain all the time.' Just really catastrophizing it and making it way worse than it actually was. I think when you're in a lot of pain that can sometimes happen, your mind really gets away from you. There's so much unknown and uncertainty, and you just don't know how long you're going to be in pain for and then you just kind of create all of this additional suffering around the issue."

She sees meditation as a solution. "When you have a meditation practice, especially like a mindfulness practice, what it will train you to do is to really, first of all, tune into the actual pain. So, with mindfulness, we're simply tuning into what's actually happening in the moment. Not everything we think we need to do about it."

Going into problem-solving mode takes you out of the moment. Wendy says, "That's the other thing with chronic pain is that you're always like, 'I should do this, I should sign up for yoga, I should go to the chiropractor, I should get this done, I should get a massage.' You can get caught up in this hamster wheel of all the things you need to do to make your pain better."

Getting out of that loop is key. "When we do a mindfulness practice, we sort of press the pause button and go, 'OK, let's just see what we're actually dealing with first.' And then you tune in and with a mindfulness practice, it's really just being present with the sensations that are actually happening, you can start to get a lot more information about your pain."

Mindfulness is also helpful for creating connection with our bodies. Wendy tells her clients who struggle with pain, "it also brings you into your body. Because a lot of us with chronic pain start to really dissociate, because it's so painful. So, you just kind of check out and long term that's not healthy either. And then the other really awesome thing that that does is it really brings you into the present moment."

Being mindful can help you focus and steak life in more manageable chunks. Wendy suggests, "I don't need to obsess over what's happened in the past, I can really just kind of be with where I'm at this moment. It just makes it so much easier to deal with instead of dealing with the next 5 to 10 years or 20 years of your life in this moment."

Mindfulness can also drive self-awareness and better information about pain, Wendy explains, "The mindfulness practice, it's such a good way to do research and get intel on yourself. As business owners, you've got so much going on. You may not have checked in and sort of like got all the information that you need about this injury or about this pain."

How to Develop a Mindfulness Practice

Once you've decided that meditation and mindfulness are good ideas, it can be hard to know where to start. It's also tough to know what can be effective and what the best way to approach it is.

Nicole Kaufman says, "The ideal time to do it is when you wake up in the morning. The reason that you want to do it then is because you are coming from delta and gamma brainwaves that are part of deep sleep. When you are crossing through that area, when you're not fully awake, but not fully asleep, you are very suggestible. That's why we read to children at the end of the evening, because when they're getting ready to go to sleep, they are drifting down from beta brainwaves into delta. We can read to kids, and they actually will get the lessons that we're saying, and that's a great time to talk to your kids too, because that's when they're highly suggestible. In the morning, it's the same thing for yourself. This is the time to plant the seeds of the vision of the person that you want to be."

She further explains, "This creative visualization time, that 20 to 30 minutes in the morning is gold. If you're not doing that then, really for most entrepreneurs that I know, chronic pain or not, you're not going to find any other time during the day to do it. There's just too much to do, there's too much distraction. Once the day gets started, it's difficult to deliberately quiet the mind, and settle into a meditative state.

When you are out of bed and have started your day, it can be too late to meditate, Nicole explains. The start of your morning routine, checking apps and devices, can derail the mental state needed for that quality meditation. Meditating before you get sucked into your day is key.

When you're a busy entrepreneur, starting a mindfulness practice can feel overwhelming. Nicole acknowledges, "Finding the time is the hardest part. Do it before you start the coffee. You won't love it at first, and it will feel tedious, especially when you are chomping at the bit to get your day started. But over time, meditating has an elegant effect on your brain. Do you remember when we used to do a "disk defrag" on old computers? Think of daily meditation as a way to disk defrag your brain in the morning, and start your day off clear-headed. Once you get into a regular practice of creative visualization/meditation each day, it will absolutely change your life, it will change your business, it will change the way you see yourself."

In terms of how much and how often, Nicole says, "The whole idea is consistency over quantity. You may have some meditations some mornings where you think about your bank account, sex, the kids, your car, or the grocery list. Some days it will be a very cool, magical kind of time. I've been doing this for five years. I've seen myself change. I've seen my business change. I've seen my level of relaxation increase."

You don't have to set up a lot of infrastructure around your new practice either. Nicole counsels that you can meditate from where you are without going on a retreat, and you can also explore yoga or tapping. Consistently using any sort of biofeedback is a great way to center oneself, a crucial practice for an entrepreneur managing chronic pain.

The hardest part is getting started and integrating this practice into your routine. If 20 to 30 minutes seems like too much (you may have to set your alarm for a bit earlier — ugh!), Nicole recommends starting with just 3 to 5 minutes of focused breathing upon waking. Commonly known as belly breathing,the practice follows an in-through- the-nose, (breathing-in-the-flowers), out through the mouth, (blow-out-the-candles) flow. That kind of breathing calms the brain, oxygenates cells, and clears your head all at the same time."

Conventional wisdom on emotional self-regulation can have gaps, Nicole counsels, "everybody says when you're under stress, just breathe. But when we register stress, the breath is the first thing that becomes dysregulated, without us ever consciously realizing it. So it makes no sense to say, 'just breathe.' It doesn't happen like that. We want to get our breathing really good in the off-stress hours. That helps bring our baseline down. And it takes more to get us triggered, more to get stressed from a lower baseline, in my opinion." A regular meditation/creative visualization practice has the ability to lower your stress level overall, so you are less triggered, less activated. She fondly refers to this state as "being able to get out of your own way."

Wendy agrees with starting small. She suggests "manageable steps and set yourself up for success. Don't start with, 'I'm going to meditate for an hour in the morning and an hour in the night for the next two weeks.' That's just unreasonable, and it's too much to go in. But you could start with, 'every time I notice my body's in pain, I'm going to stop and pay attention to it.'"

That can look all sorts of ways, but she suggests, "I'm going to spend one minute paying attention to where the pain is and what it feels like. If you did that for three weeks, or even a week, you'll probably start to really notice things. The other best way to get started is hands down, by far, get a teacher and study with a community. It makes such a difference."

You don't have to go it alone, Wendy explains, "If you study with a teacher too, they'll be able to just really expedite the process. When you're practicing at-home meditation, there can be lots of distractions. But when you sign up for a class, or go study with a teacher, there [are] no distractions, you can meditate for way longer, you get way more out of it. I just find that human connection just makes it so much easier too."

How do you know what practice to start with? Wendy suggests, "I have found that the mindfulness techniques or the Mindfulness Based Stress Reduction, they're the best way to start. But also, go to whatever you're drawn to. Some people really love visualizations, some people really love chakra meditations. So, if you love it, there's going to be a way higher chance of you being successful with it. Follow what you're excited about."

On picking a teacher, Wendy says, "Look for someone who has a meditation practice and has been meditating for a significant amount of time. I think it's really good to find someone that you connect with. If you love intellectual discussions, find a meditation teacher that's trained at a master's degree or a PhD level. If you're not intellectual, and you don't like that kind of thing, find someone that's doing something different that uses the kind of language that you understand."

You also have to do your homework. "It's good to look for some level of professionalism. See if they've been around for a while, see if they've been teaching for a while, if they have a community. If you have meditation teachers that are telling you, 'this is the only way, this is what you need to do. Don't do anything else. Study with me all the time.' For me, that's a warning sign, go somewhere else."

However you decide to explore mindfulness, it's important to create space for it in your business. It will help you build your business and to take better care of yourself. The benefits of meditation have been well-researched and it's an evidence-based way to help yourself feel better and deal with the big feelings that come with chronic pain.

There are so many courses of action that well-intentioned people suggest to help manage pain that are not rooted in science. Meditation and mindfulness are choices that are documented to be helpful. If you give it a chance, it could really make a difference. Don't just do something, sit there!

Develop Your Coping Toolbox

Part of developing your coping toolbox is having a game plan for when the big feelings hit. Hilary Jastram says, "I think like a huge part of this journey has to do with acceptance. It's very, very hard to accept that this is me. Sometimes I want somebody to just crawl in bed with me and stroke my hair and tell me "It does suck, and I'm so sorry," but to not stay there, there needs to be parameters."

Hilary talks about setting boundaries around how long you're going to indulge yourself. she talks about how she practices this herself, "I'll be like, Hey, listen, this sucks and you can have the rest of today to feel sucky about it. You can cry, you can watch bad Lifetime movies, you can wallow. But tomorrow, you're going to get up and you're going to try as hard as you can. Because maybe wallowing in that day for that moment, is the best that you can do. Maybe that's your best day that day. And that's OK. But you're not going to live there. I'm going to acknowledge these feelings. And then I'm also going to make the commitment to move forward.'

Hilary believes that you have to take responsibility for that moving forward and speaks to the consequences if you don't. "What's going to come from that is you're going to have a hard time moving forward. You're going to stay there and you're going to lose out on opportunities."

Ultimately what it comes down to is resilience and building inner strength. You need to learn how to manage these big feelings when they come up because they will. Every challenge, every struggle, every time you can't easily achieve something is a reminder that there is something that is hard and legitimately stressful that is threatening to hold you back. You need to find your footing so you can keep going. That starts from within.

Build an Arsenal of the Things That Make You Feel Better

The things that can be helpful in making us feel better when we're dealing with chronic pain can vary widely from person to person. It's important to look at what helps you when you're struggling and find ways to integrate that into your life.

A great starting point is to finding the smallest step you can take to feel better. You don't have to renovate your entire life; you can find just one thing that helps. Tomorrow you can try to find another thing. There isn't a race when it comes to self-care and it's perfectly reasonable to take your time and experiment.

Danielle Christopher's advice was, "Go take a walk outside, go just breathe. Take a sip of water. Take five … that's been our biggest thing this year is take that five minutes, reset, and then it's much easier to get back to. It's all the rational stuff we know but we don't do."

For me it looks like hitting the snooze button for nine more minutes of lying there and being mindful. It's daily baths and using my CPAP machine to ensure that I get appropriate sleep. I try to drink plenty of water to stay hydrated and spend time on the water to relax and feel at peace.

"I wish I [had] started focusing on how movement affects pain at an earlier stage," Lana Welchman admitted.

Exercise

Exercise is one good way to manage pain. It can be a distraction from the drudgery of daily demands that come from a sore body. Completing a particularly difficult workout can build self-efficacy. You realize you can do that and then you start looking for the next thing you can conquer.

Sheila Sutherland says, "It comes down to what we are tolerating in our life that we've become numb to. I got really numb to the tightness, the tension, the stress that my body was constantly under. Getting out in nature was a big thing for me. Even though I may only be able physically to do a 10-minute walk, or some days, I may be able to do a 45-minute walk. During the whole COVID time, almost every day, I was out in nature somewhere. That's what helped me cope with a lot of the stress. We know, when stressors go up, our chronic pain escalates exponentially. I had to be proactive with that."

Endorphins can be really helpful for mood stability and that is something that you can make happen with regular exercise. Similarly, sweating out the stress can be helpful also. It's about finding an outlet that works for you.

In my experience, the exercise that you're going to do regularly tends to be the exercise that you enjoy, and creating movement habits for ongoing mood stability can go a long way.

Amanda Knapper found comfort in her regular walks. "We go for a walk once a day, which I insist on and we make time for, because I need the exercise and to exercise that limb and it also helps me sleep."

Finding time

Making time can certainly be a challenge. It's one that Jen Campbell encounters as she's coaching women but she always takes the time to dig deeper. "When I'm working with women, and they say I don't have time to exercise, I want to know how much they're on social media in the day."

She explains, "I don't want to shame people for it. I know that there's a reason we go on social media, I know a lot of people are looking for connections, they're looking to numb, they're looking to check out of their very stressful and overwhelming lives. But we get in these cycles, where we pursue behaviors to check out of our lives. But those behaviors perpetuate the cycle of us feeling more and more behind in our lives."

The scrolling snowball

It's a slippery slope and easy to find yourself on the wrong side of the balanced equation for time spent scrolling. Jen illustrates what happens with too much screen time, "So if there are people spending three hours a day on social media, while the laundry piles up, these boring self-care items pile up, and they and it becomes a vicious cycle of avoidance, numbing, avoidance, numbing, and then we're having breakdowns, so there's going to be people out there who don't have time, there will, but there's a whole heck of a lot in that gray zone area, who are not intentionally deciding where they want to spend their time."

Focusing on What Matters

This over-dependence on social media and numbing behaviors is problematic because it gets in the way of wellness activities that can really make a difference. Jen Campbell says, "Exercise is the one of the most impactful habits anyone can do for their physical and, often, mental health. When people tell me, "I don't have time to exercise," I want to know, 'Where are you spending your time?'"

This time-management challenge has broader implications. Jen explains, "A lot of people spend their time in places they wish they wouldn't. They're pushing discomfort forward. They're choosing to stay comfortable in the moment but they're not dealing with these more uncomfortable aspects."

Jen uses an easy visual to help relay the challenge that comes from too much time on devices. "You're like a snowplow just like this in the snow is just piling up, that's how I see numbing behaviors and choosing self-care that it feels really good in the moment."

Too Much of a Good Thing Can Be a Bad Thing

It's not black and white, Jen Campbell says, "I see it as this self-care this continuum, self-care on one side and self-harm on the other. The longer you go, the longer you spend doing some of these behaviors, you start sliding on that scale into self-harm. So, you want to watch Netflix for two hours one night, totally do it, go for it, it feels good. I love it personally. You want to watch Netflix for two days. You are in major self-harm territory, unless you really have nothing else to do. But for most of us, we become that snowplow."

Sometimes to deal with these maladaptive behaviors and patterns getting outside help can be productive. There are situations where you need an outside perspective to help you get back on track. There is no shame in asking for help and what help looks like might vary from person to person. It's all about assembling your pit crew — that could be finding a coach or therapist. They sound like the same thing but they are not. They each have their own benefits and goals.

The Benefits of Therapy

Therapy can be tremendously helpful in dealing with life stress, stabilizing emotions, and learning valuable skills for self-regulation. It can also be helpful in managing chronic pain. Therapist Meagan Hamilton explained what works best for therapy and chronic pain.

"There are two techniques that come to mind. One is looking at old events or things that happened, which might be contributing to current pain levels. So Eye Movement Desensitization and Reprocessing (EMDR) is certainly a wonderful tool, a therapy technique to support people with chronic pain and resolve some of that 'old stuff' that might be contributing to current (problem) pain. The other technique, which is one of my favorites, is looking at rewriting thoughts to interpret pain and/or side effects of pain."

The way we think about our pain can have an impact. Meagan shares, "I often use an analogy of a knob. The pain is going to be there. But it's learning to turn it down. Some people find it really helpful to look at reinterpreting how we're experiencing pain, as well as looking at behaviors that we do when we are having pain, which might contribute to further poor mood."

But how do you know if therapy is the right process for you? Meagan offered these signs that could be worth checking what professional help could do for you, such as "feeling quite stuck, or probably one of the main things that comes to mind is, if people say things like, 'my pain is bad every day, or my pain is always there, or pain is getting in the way of everything that's making me happy, or getting in the way of achieving my goals.'"

Those kinds of blanket statements need to be addressed. Meagan shared, "I certainly might work with somebody on a one-to-one level to really look at rating pain, multiple times a day to really look at, while pain is really causing you a lot of grief, it's not actually impacting you for the entire day. Maybe it's worse in the morning, or it's worse at night. But there are still some moments where you can flourish or achieve your goals and it's not totally taking over."

While that difference might seem inconsequential, it can actually have a big impact. Meagan explains, "We can get really stuck in that negative self-talk loop of how pain is ruining our lives and sure it's certainly impacting them, but for most, not every moment of every day is pain a ten out of ten."

The Benefits of Coaching

Life coach Aryn Savard talked about the benefits of coaching from a problem-solving and mindset-shifting perspective. "I think one of the most valuable things when it comes to coaches is the ability to shift perspective. Oftentimes we are in the "me" perspective and a coach can help you look outside yourself from a larger perspective. One of the ways I do this is introducing curiosity instead of outcome. Asking questions like, "what are you curious about? What is possible?"

In terms of the role of the coach, Aryn explained, "It's not that a coach knows better than you or has all the answers. It's just that they have a different perspective. They help your connect with the truth within by looking at challenges from a fresh prespective."

High-performance coach Teri Holland talked about her coaching methodologies from a neuro-linguistic programming (NLP) perspective. "The one thing that I teach my clients, and this comes from NLP, and it's a little bit different than traditional coaching, is that for chronic pain to exist in the body, there has to be a level of dissociation from our emotions."

In terms of how she coaches clients through that, Teri explains, "Where some people might talk about separating themselves from the pain, I teach my clients that you need to address the feelings that are underneath it. Instead of detaching from it or trying to separate yourself, because chronic pain, really essentially, from our perspective in NLP, from the unconscious mind, it's like a five-year-old tugging on your sleeve saying 'pay attention, pay attention to what you're feeling, what are your emotions?'"

But how can you tell if coaching is needed? Teri suggests, "If you're feeling overwhelmed, there're too many plates spinning and you can't keep them all going anymore. Feeling like, 'I keep setting the same goal, and I'm not achieving the goal. I keep striving for that same level of success. And I never seem to get there, I always seem to hit an obstacle and can never seem to push through.' That's a good indicator. Or the client who says, 'I keep achieving all my goals, and

I'm burnt out and I'm exhausted.' That's another good indication that coaching is needed. 'I can't keep up this momentum. I can't keep going at this pace. I'm done.'"

On picking a coach, Teri suggests, "I'm a fan of certifications. That's always a controversial topic in the coaching world. My thinking around it is that anyone who's truly a professional in what they do is going to take the time to educate themselves and become trained and qualified in what they're doing. I don't think a piece of paper necessarily means that person's the best coach, but it means they've at least taken the time to learn their craft. So, the first thing I would look at is are they qualified? Do they have a certification? I wouldn't hire a plumber to come unclog the drain in my house who isn't certified and trained. So, I definitely wouldn't hire someone who's going to work on my business or my mind or my life who doesn't have some qualifications behind them."

Success beyond certification is something else Teri suggests looking at. "Depending on what area you want coaching in, if it's coaching for business, look at someone who's had some business success. If it's relationship coaching … do they have a healthy relationship? If it's, you know, I had a client come to me and he'd worked with a previous coach. He was going to coach him on wealth strategies, but then he found out he lived in this tiny little basement apartment and hadn't achieved wealth on his own, well, how is he going to then coach his client on wealth? So, look at the credibility — you want someone who walks the talk and practices what they preach."

Finally, Teri suggests looking at your personal connection to the coach, "How do you feel with that person? Do you have good rapport with them? Are you able to open up and talk to them? Do you feel like it's a safe environment to talk and do you feel supported by this person?"

Jen Campbell agrees that coaching can be helpful under the right circumstances. "When I think coaching can be valuable for someone living with a chronic pain condition is when they have coaching that understands that and also really understands this all or nothing mindset that so many people have."

She suggests working with a coach and looking at, "Here is what is nonnegotiable, because I live with this. But here's what is negotiable. Here's what I can do and what I'm willing to do. Everybody has to look at the limitations of their own circumstance and look at,

'What am I willing to do inside of this circumstance? What am I not willing to do?'"

While chronic pain can be a challenge, there are still things that you can do to improve your wellness. Jen says, "You live with chronic pain, but you can still shut your phone off earlier at night. We get into these mindsets of, 'I'm struggling with this. What can you do?' And that's what coaching is. That's where I think coaching and therapy can really differ, is that therapy is often like a deep dive. A coach's job is to keep you in motion. An object in motion stays in motion. It is a coach's job to continue to nudge you along and move forward and find ways around these barriers that you experience and trouble-shoot with you."

As part of exploring what is going to be helpful you need to determine what it is that you're actually looking for in terms of support. Jen spoke of her own experiences as a coach and how you need to be "really getting clear on 'do you need therapy, or do you need a coach, or do you need a bit of both?' I find with my coaching experience that I'm often just helping women organize their brains and get their priorities lined up in a way that is aligned with their values and their wellness vision for themselves."

The reality is that while we struggle with these challenges individually, they do have an impact on our relationships. That is something that we need to keep in mind as we design our work-life balance and take stock of the areas we need intervention.

Making Time for the People Who Matter

While a lot of the work that we have to do to withstand chronic pain happens inside, it can be greatly improved through social contact and through positive relationships with others. The flexibility of entrepreneurship doesn't guarantee improved relationships. You have to actually do the work in order to achieve better relationships and these relationships are integral to your wellness as you navigate entrepreneurship with chronic pain.

Jake Schaap reinforces how valuable support is. "I really think that it is absolutely needed for anyone with autoimmune disease or chronic illness to surround themselves with a support system. You need a team or people around you to be able to support you, that have your back, that understand your goals and your mission, to be able to just move your mission forward, when you cannot physically do it yourself."

It's not just entrepreneurs with chronic pain who need support though. Jake says, "I think that is super needed for anyone I mean, in general, you need a team to be successful in business, regardless of if you're sick or not. But especially when you're sick, you can't control your symptoms, or your flare-ups or whatever you need, you need support around you to be able to move that mission and network forward for you."

Getting intentional about your relationships is something that is much needed in order to ensure that they are healthy. Danielle Christopher shared one of her challenges around her role as a mom navigating business with chronic pain. "My youngest had some pictures show up on her iPad, it was the back of my head doing this on the computer. That's what she saw and I went, 'Oh my God. That's not good. Like, that's all that I'm doing.'"

While she understood why she was doing it, it wasn't what she wanted. "That actually was a big wakeup call going, 'OK, time to put it down now.' Because also then we don't want them to be on screens. So, if I'm on a screen doing emailing that's what they see, me modeling that behavior. So, I'm really conscious of going, 'OK, if I'm advocating screen-free time, I need to do that.'"

Part of getting intentional about relationships requires structure and ongoing commitment.

Hilary Jastram shares how she and her husband make it work. "One thing that I do not compromise on is dinner with my husband every single night. I don't take calls then, and that's final. It takes work and commitment every single day."

Dana Corey focuses not just on the how but also the who, explaining, "The number one thing I do for my pain is make sure that the people around me are funny. The thing about laughter is that it doesn't make the pain go away, but it makes it tolerable."

Beyond humor, she also looks for people with whom she can be authentic, encouraging. "Make sure that you have at least one person around you who you could be really open and honest with and tell them how much it hurts and a person who won't make you feel less than. That it's just pain. It's not you."

Meagan Hamilton is a big proponent of community and its power. She says, "Connect with other entrepreneurs. Don't work in a silo. Working in isolation is not the most effective. Maybe your field or niche is quite narrow and so you think you cannot connect or relate to other people. That's simply not true. There are other people, other businesses out there."

She underscores how valuable those relationships can be. "Connection is really healthy, really important, and will foster that whole idea of balance. That's really important. I think as entrepreneurs, we think of a lot of late nights at the kitchen table with our computer. And that can be true, and it doesn't have to be. Connection is going to help keep us in check."

No entrepreneur is an island. We need people to support us, whether we are healthy or well. So often we pursue running our own business to have more time for people but when we aren't intentional about making time for them, the relationships we hoped would deepen get lost in the shuffle.

Surrounding yourself with the right people can help you find satisfaction in your business and your life and when it comes to having a good laugh, a spoonful of sugar makes the medicine go down, just like Mary Poppins says.

Write Your Way Out

As I spoke with entrepreneurs while in development of this book, a theme that kept coming up for dealing with pain effectively was journaling. I expected to see a combination of journaling, art, and music therapy but what I found was that journaling was one of the most popular ways to deal with the big feelings associated with chronic pain.

Jake Schaap explained how journaling helped him understand himself, "It's like me looking at myself from a third-party perspective. At the time when I'm writing I'm usually at a heightened state of emotion. When I go back to read what I've written I'm not in that mental state anymore. I can see what has set me off or what hasn't set me off, 'Why did I react to this thing?' I'm able to kind of have that conversation with myself and see different parts of myself. You can better understand like, 'OK, if this happens next time, then I reacted this way last time, how can I make it better?'"

Sarah Hosseini, a journaling coach, had tips on how to use journaling to manage chronic pain.

"The first thing that you can do is break out the journal and emotionally dump about it. If you're having a really bad, chronic pain day, you're going to break out that journal and get all of the ranting, the raw, the jagged stuff out of you."

She explains why doing so is so important. "Getting that emotional dump, it does a couple of things. It affirms what you're feeling. The other thing that it's doing, which is really cool is when you're journaling, and you're slowing down, and you're writing with pen and paper, your brain basically de-intensifies those really strong feelings that you're having in the moment, and helps you emotionally regulate around chronic pain. Just the act of that, it slows down your brain, de-intensifies the emotion, which has been proven to de-intensify the pain."

Manage your expectations (and your symptoms)

Sarah Hosseini cautions to manage expectations about the outcomes of journaling, "I'm not talking about journaling being the cure to chronic illness at all. But there's some cool science behind the fact that it helps you regulate and manage your symptoms better just in the act of acknowledging it and talking about it to your journal."

Connect with your body more deeply

Journaling can also help you build body awareness. Sarah Hosseini says, "It helps you do a body scan, almost like a check in, because it's a slower process. It's this moment with yourself that you can take a body scan and really tap into, 'OK, where is the area that I'm hurting most? OK, this is the area, I need to then make a list in my journal that I'm going to focus on or I'm going to tell my healer to focus on.'"

Get clearer about what's going on

Having that level of attention and insight can be helpful in managing your condition. Sarah Hosseini explains, "By journaling about your chronic pain and where it's physically manifesting specifically helps you get specific in your healing and what you're going to do for it."

Learn to accept yourself

The impacts are not just physical but also emotional Sarah Hosseini relays, "The other thing that it does is journaling helps you go deep into the chronic pain and identify an emotional component that most people ignore or don't accept. Journaling about chronic illness also cultivates acceptance within yourself."

That level of acceptance can lead to taking better action to advocate for yourself. Sarah shared her personal experience, "I find if you journal about your chronic illness, it actually helps you to lean into it and be like, 'OK, this is something that I do have, this is something that I want to talk about. And this is something that yes, I can still do my job, but maybe I need to do it differently. Maybe I need an accommodation.'"

Spending time with your journal can help you get clear on your priorities. Sarah talks about how "journaling helps identify, for a person who suffers from chronic illness, what situations and what jobs they're willing to tolerate, or not tolerate and get really clear on that instead of being shamed into just taking all these pills and muscle through it."

Track your habits, change your life

More than just a treatment option, journaling is also prevention. Sarah Hosseini talks about how the practice can be used to dial in on habits and actions that could be helping or hindering us. "Journaling helps you identify the possible reason for the flare-up. Were you under more stress? Did you not sleep that well? We all know that journaling is not going to cure chronic illness. But, I mean, it's helpful."

Journaling isn't the silver bullet that will take down chronic pain, but it can help you manage, understand, and prevent it to a certain extent. Writing is a highly effective tool in your coping toolbox and it's one worth exploring. Carrying everything inside isn't healthy, and you need to find ways to release your big feelings into the world. Try journaling and see what a difference it can make.

9

FIND JOY IN THE JOURNEY

Just because it's hard, doesn't mean it has to feel hard. Rewiring yourself for positivity can help you find more joy. I'm not talking about "good vibes only" toxic positivity; I'm talking about setting yourself up for success from a mood perspective by being intentional about what you do and how you think about things.

Tim Salau talks about how he finds joy. "Every day is really day one. I think a lot of entrepreneurs need to stop operating with a scarcity mindset. They need to start operating with an abundance mindset and I think for me a lot of my joy and enthusiasm comes from my abundance mindset and the fact that I know that as an entrepreneur there will always be a customer that is willing to be a part of our movement. Why? Because customers believe in companies and people that exude joy, that want to do good in the world."

Sometimes that joy comes from meaning. Tim says, "Too many entrepreneurs give up. They give up and they don't feel as if they can do it, they're always operating with limiting beliefs, they let everyone else get in their head, and they don't have their own chutzpah or their own conviction on where they want to take their lives or their business. It's more important how you want to create impact. I think the conviction a founder or an entrepreneur has is really quite important actually that's because that's the joy that keeps you going when it's tough."

For me, in my journey finding joy, it isn't about always being happy or always looking on the bright side, it's more about noticing the mess and finding peace regardless. It's about changing your to-do list into a list of how you want to feel and finding ways to curate experiences to create that. That doesn't have to be an elaborate process, it can be as simple as a hot coffee on a cold day or a brisk walk in the evening air.

Not every day is going to be a good day but every day you show up to will have some good in it because you were there.

Why Gratitude Matters

Gratitude is something that Tim Salau centers in his perspective. He says, "As you go through this journey of being a founder and entrepreneur, every day is not going to be happy, every day is not joy, the reality is that every day is a grind, and you have to be grateful for that."

He takes an "every day is day one" perspective and explains, "The whole notion of a day one is that, what would you do on day one that you say you're proud of? Did you build your company? Did you take one step further? OK good, then do it again tomorrow. Do it again the day after, every day is day one."

All of those efforts add up, according to Tim, "By the time you realize it by day 5,000, it's still day one, but you have a billion-dollar business, or more importantly you have a billion customers that that's the mindset we need. We need founders and entrepreneurs to embrace that mindset, because when they embrace that mindset, they'll feel much more successful in a venture that they're building, and they'll see much more success in their lives. Every single day is day one."

Life coach Aryn Savard talked about her own gratitude practice. "Being in a space of gratitude, for me, is about being present with what is, not being thankful for things or people. It's about seeing things with an honest lens, whether we think they are good or bad and seeing the gift in it all, from a higher perspective."

Wendy Kapty-Weymann has her own perspective on the power of gratitude and why it's so important, explaining, "Gratitude practices shift everything. I have noticed this over and over again. When you're in chronic pain there's so many things to be negative about. There's so many things to complain about and it's so hard."

How gratitude affects the brain

The power of gratitude isn't just a feel-good concept, there's real science behind it. Kim Strobel says, "What we know is that gratitude is one of the top five research-based ways that a person can raise their baseline happiness level. We all have a baseline happiness level, and it goes up, and it goes down. But it almost always returns to baseline. If you incorporate a two-minute daily practice into your life called gratitude, then what happens is after 21 days of practicing writing down three different things every day that you are thankful for, that we actually can begin to rewire the brain."

It's really about being intentional with your thoughts. Kim explains, "The average human being has about 70,000 thoughts a day. The average human being, about 80 percent of those thoughts are negative, which means most of us are going around every day and we've had about 56,000 negative thoughts." That's a lot of negativity to wade through on top of being in pain.

It's not really our fault though, our brains were built this way. Kim explains why the structure of the brain shapes our perceptions, "Part of our brain, our amygdala, was really wired to be on the alert for any kind of negative activity, danger, threats, all of that. [In primitive times], we didn't know if there was a saber-toothed tiger or a clan of people that was going to come in and wipe us out. Or would we have shelter that would keep us from freezing to death."

Our brains are just doing what they were supposed to do, she clarifies, "Our brains' number one job is to scan its environment for negativity or danger. The problem is that today, we still have the amygdala, and it still operates that way, even though most of us are not in constant danger."

So how do you overcome that? Kim explains the research on gratitude. "What we know is that if you can jot down these three different things every day, for 21 days, you create a new neural feedback loop in your brain. When you create that new neural feedback loop, your brain then begins to scan its environment, and things that are going well start to pop out a lot more than all that's going wrong.

It's just really simple practice. It takes two minutes a day, but it really is a game changer in our lives."

Choosing gratitude gives you something different to focus on instead of just praying. It intentionally redirects your brain from the negative experience of pain into something more positive. Gratitude for what we have gives us room to hope for something better in the future.

Gratitude shapes perspectives but it also enriches relationships. As we know, relationships are really important when you have chronic pain and otherwise, and Kim talks about how gratitude can be a game-changer in your connections. "Whatever we focus on grows. There was a time when I focused heavily on all of the things that I didn't think that [my husband] did [well] enough. I would complain about those things. And in my head, I would do a lot of negative self-talk about those things. Then I started to notice more things that I felt like he was not doing well or enough in our relationship."

There's a way to shift that and get out of that pattern of negativity. Kim suggests, "Really try to think of the things that your partner is doing that you really appreciate. Not only that but take the time to tell them. We actually know from John Gottman, in his research at the Gottman Institute out there that when partners can show verbal appreciation for one another that starts to grow. You start to notice more things about that partner that you really enjoy."

Building a gratitude practice for yourself, your life, and your relationship with others can involve journaling. In order to start building that gratitude journaling practice, Sarah Hosseini has some ideas. She says, "It's going to be really important even those moments where you feel like you can't focus on the good things, you're going to have to really push yourself in your journaling and usually when you have the journal in front of you, celebrating your wins."

The brain can help turn a disadvantage into an advantage. Sarah says, "Mindset is everything with chronic illness so many times, it really helps shift the mindset to say, 'This is not the thing I'm failing at. This is the thing that I'm winning at still. I'm not weak in this way. This is how I'm strong.'"

Beyond her expertise as a coach it's something she's experienced firsthand in her own health journey. "With my endometriosis, if I have some days where I'm in bed, I used to feel really bad. I can't play with my kids, or my kids see me like this, and I feel really weak or I feel really guilty that I'm not there for them."

Gratitude is something that helps shift that experience for her. "But then going back to the journal and having gratitude about, 'I was able to work from my bed today. My kids were invited into my bed to watch a movie, and I got that quality time with them.' Just simple stuff like that. It helps you cope with all of the negativity and shift the mindset."

Work-Life Integration versus Work-Life Balance

There's a lot of talk about whether we should be pursuing work-life integration or work-life balance. However you frame it, what's most important is that you build something that works for you. Pain is something that you have to deal with and spending the majority of your time either focused on pain or work doesn't leave a lot of room for the rest of your life. There's so much more to life than pain and work.

Amanda Knapper recommends that you "be aware of yourself and your pain and what you're capable of. Push yourself by all means but remember to be aware and cognizant of what limitations and what strategies you have to take to make it better. For me, it's always about realizing that I have to take time. If I have to take time away from work, just to deal with what I'm dealing with, then I will do it. Sometimes I just chug through. But usually when it's a headache in the back of my head where I'm like, 'OK, well, let's get what I have to get done, done and then stop.' And I do so."

You need to create boundaries around your work time and energy. Danielle Christopher says, "Make sure you're still having fun. If you're not having fun, rethink the next chapter. Knowing when to shut off the office hours was my biggest, hugest thing to learn."

It wasn't as simple as making a decision to work less. It took some time. It isn't just for you but also to provide consistency for your clients, Danielle explains, "Five o'clock, you're all out of office ... setting that time and sticking to it. Don't be emailing at ten o'clock at night. Because then once clients know you're available, they'll keep calling and expecting you to call back."

Danielle didn't have to implement this change on her own, she had help. "It helps having my husband as my partner because we police each other. Having my best friend as my business partner definitely helps." Because they're in business together and are also life partners, Danielle and her husband held each other accountable for creating balance.

Kim Strobel sees the impact of not creating balance in her coaching practice all the time, "Women are used to not putting themselves at the top of their list. I always tell people and teach that you are not selfish for putting yourself first some of the time. You are allowed to be more than a mother and more than a spouse or a partner, even while you're going through that. What happens is women lose their souls because they become everything to everyone else, and they don't know that they're allowed to count along the way."

Just like we need to be intentional about creating space for our relationships, we also need to be intentional about creating time for ourselves. Kim suggests a solution, "I honestly think that a woman should create space every single day in her life that is just for her. If that seems impossible, then I tell people to start out with one 15-minute spot. But the problem is women fill their calendar up with all their commitments, and then they look for holes to see, 'Hey, when can I get my me time in?' They're not prioritizing themselves."

The root of the difficulty in finding that time is a matter of priority. Kim shares how she puts herself first. "I go first on my calendar, and then I fill in around that because I have some nonnegotiables in my life, because I know what it takes to keep Kim Strobel healthy."

We often are not putting ourselves first. It's all so easy to fall into the trap of comparison. Kim explains why what other people need shouldn't matter when we are evaluating what we need ourselves.

"That's the other thing we do is we compare, right? Kim Strobel needs 45 minutes of exercise six days a week, she needs a weekly massage. She needs time alone. Then there's somebody else like my friend Trish, who doesn't ever need a massage and probably doesn't even need 45 minutes of exercise. Maybe she needs a lot less to feel happy and content."

Kim turns her focus from what other people need to what she needs to be happy. "I don't care. I'm not her. I'm me. I have to decide what that mental health looks like for me. I know what Kim needs to be her best, and then give myself permission to bring that into my life."

Sheila Sutherland creates balance by not overscheduling herself. "Instead of having this stocked calendar, I have to build in 'nothing' days. And I call them my nothing days because it's OK if I'm in my pajamas all day. I don't have to be anywhere, it can just be whatever that day develops into. There's no expectation for myself. I'll have other days where I've got some high expectations, but I have to balance between the two or else I crash. And then I'm off for two or three weeks and what good is that?"

We also have to give ourselves grace to change our minds. Sheila talks about the struggle she faces with not always being able to predict if she will feel well enough to do what she planned. "I get tired of explaining myself to my friends and family. I really work on trying to get them to understand that I may agree to do something on Monday. But by Friday, I don't know how I'm going to feel. So, if I do have to do a last-minute cancellation, do not take it personally."

She thinks it's also about being honest with yourself about what you can do, and that it's all about "knowing what your expectations are, and really monitoring them to make sure they're realistic. Are they realistic to who I was before the pain? Or are they realistic to who I am now? Unfortunately, that's two different people. If you deny the pain, it finds the way to show up twice as much, if not more."

Jenny Kanevsky found her ability to create balance through her pricing structure and by identifying her clients more appropriately. "I made a commitment to myself that I was going to work less and make more money. I targeted a higher-end client." She was able to do this because she took pride in her abilities. "I recognized the value that I brought to the table that wasn't just 'Oh, I'm a good content writer,' but I bring 25 years of marketing experience and a graduate degree, and everything that I bring to the table, all of that combined is really valuable, and I'm going to charge for it."

When she focused on her own value, she was able to let go of the guilt of charging more money for her services, explaining, "I'm not going to feel bad about it. In order to make the amount of money that I want to make and not have to work as many hours, this is what I'm going to have to do to get there."

For Jenny, it wasn't just about charging enough, it was also about guarding her energy by being strategic about who she worked with. She knows that "working with clients who stress you out, for whatever reason, who aren't your ideal client, that's going to exacerbate your pain."

Dana Corey has had to take action as well in order to create balance for herself and find happiness. "I've taken serious, committed, and ongoing steps to make sure that I don't work too much."

Jen Campbell encourages focus to create balance. "You have to get very intentional as an entrepreneur [as far as] where you are willing to spend your time. Now, I coach women and some of them are entrepreneurs, some of them are not. But the distractions that we all have in our lives are universal, whether you're an entrepreneur or not. When I say protect your brain, I think beyond entrepreneurship, just living a meaningful, intentional life. As an entrepreneur, time and money are their biggest, most precious resource. Lots of entrepreneurs would say time more than money."

Sherry Edmunds-Flett talks about balance on the impact it has on chronic pain when we fall out of balance. "If we don't have some kind of balance, then we're hooped. It's especially important for those of us who do have a chronic illness because if we don't have or attempt or work at balance, then we're going to be even hooped even further than those people that see themselves as healthy."

The reality is that when you have chronic pain you have more demands on your attention and more things on your to-do list. Nicole Kaufman says, "You have two businesses, you have the business of dealing with your pain, you have the business of dealing with your business. So, you're really having two businesses and the urge to work endlessly as an entrepreneur, because there's always work to do, there's always something you can be doing, right? Listening to your body and conscious self-regulation are paramount for those struggling with chronic pain. Harnessing this power will be the difference between you managing your illness, or your illness managing you."

That constant availability of work is something Meagan Hamilton is conscious of. "As an entrepreneur, we're 'on' all the time. I sometimes will catch myself having conversations with people and be thinking about 'Oh this is a great idea; how can I incorporate this into the work I'm doing?' And then I have to remember, 'you're out with a friend, this is your visit, you're with a friend, work mode and play mode/home mode are two different things.' And so, practicing and noticing that that might be our default, and bringing it back. And it's just practice."

Balance is a practice that we build over time and Meagan encourages clients to commit to the process. "I think the more we can practice that and have awareness with that, and normalize that as an entrepreneur, the healthier we will be and having that balance, I think we can get really hooked into this, like "hustle and grind it out" this, the entrepreneurial culture. And it can be really motivating and intoxicating in some ways, but it's also really unhealthy if we really adopt it in its purest form."

Ultimately, she encourages people to come back to their purpose. She says that because "that's not why people start their own business and become entrepreneurs. They do it because they want balance, they want to have say in how they spend their time. So, this grind it out, go, go, go. I mean, even the toughest metals will break; with enough pressure they will bend. So, we have to kind of think about that. It's not sustainable."

That isn't to say that entrepreneurs don't have to work hard. Meagan acknowledges, "There are certainly going to be moments where we need to be putting in extra time or certain projects that or even with COVID, or life situations that might be busier. But it's recognizing, at what point do I need to tap out? Or practice some downtime and balance?"

Teri Holland encourages people to be realistic to create balance, "I think a big part of it is setting boundaries and recognizing what's possible to do and then being really clear on where the boundaries are and learning to say 'no.' I dealt with a chronic illness for 23 years and a big part of me learning to run my business and deal with it was learning how to say no to things."

Those boundaries aren't just for entrepreneurs with chronic pain, Teri explains. "I think that's something that every entrepreneur needs to learn, but especially if you're dealing with chronic pain, it's becoming very, very clear on what those boundaries are and being confident to uphold those boundaries and say 'no,' and not 'no, I can't' or 'no, I'm sorry,' but just 'no, I'm not doing that or not taking that on.'"

On the subject of time management, Teri offers, "If you know that your body can handle, say, this window of time a day where you can be really productive, then that's where you focus in and that becomes a priority."

Creating your perfect day is an exercise that you can use to create your vision for the balance that you want in your life. I've taken time to really think about what my day would look like with balance, what kinds of things I might do on a daily basis and really think through moment-to-moment what a balanced day would look like.

When you're shooting for this big concept of balance without any specifics it can be really hard to know when you've achieved it. By getting detailed about what balance means to you, you have a better sense of when you're achieving it and when you are still struggling. Having a model of a day of balance to aim for lets you focus your efforts more intentionally and build the kind of life that you want to live, ultimately.

All Work and No Play: Rediscovering Play

I discovered the importance of play over the course of the pandemic. I felt a lot of guilt for feeling the way that I did, because so many people were struggling, and I felt badly that the lack of play in my life was something that I was concerned about.

I saw it as a sign of my privilege and I felt badly that while people were out of work, I was concerned about not being playful enough. But the reality is that play can help us work through big emotions and it can help us create balance. Play can be therapeutic when you're dealing with trauma and in the case of a pandemic or the experience of chronic pain, there is a lot of trauma to process.

Life coach and pole dance studio owner Aryn Savard talked about when she realized how important play was for her wellness. "I hit a pretty severe depression when I was 39. And I realized that it's because I was forgetting to play. I was so deep into my work and business. As much as I loved pole, it was still my business. Instead of me going and playing in it, I was just teaching and immersing myself in the business aspect of things."

She found a way to turn it around for herself by getting back to her roots of play. "I started setting aside some time on Fridays, just for my own exploration and play in the studio. That was huge in terms of my inspiration and letting go of that weight of being responsible every time I walked into my studio. It let me just explore, play, express, and be whatever I needed to be at the time."

For Aryn, it was also about exploring play outside the context of what she did in her business. "I also got back into scuba diving. And that was a big one for me. I realized how much I loved the ocean and how much I hadn't prioritized that as my play."

There are lots of ways to add playfulness to your day, whether it involves putting on music while you're cooking, dancing in the kitchen, or spending time exploring hobbies. Setting an intention to play is powerful. It's about looking at what you have to do and finding ways to make them fun.

Writing this book was a real challenge for me and the only way that I got through it was finding ways to make it fun. In the final weekend where I was writing, I created an experience for myself to finish off my book. I ordered my favorite foods, and I spent time exploring whether I'm a wax melt person by using a warmer and a selection of waxes that I purchased.

It felt silly at the time, but I did playful things to create the energy I wanted to bring to my writing session. I wanted to show up with my most confident self and in order to do that I had to play. I did my hair and makeup and I dressed up nicely just for myself. It didn't have to be for anyone else, it was fun, and it was a way to stimulate my creativity to help me execute the creative work at hand.

Having chronic pain is hard work, and integrating play helps offset that burden and allows you to create enjoyment in your life. When pain happens so frequently, it's important to focus on creating space for enjoyable experiences. Playing can be part of staying healthy if it keeps you feeling positive and hopeful.

10
PUT IT ALL TOGETHER

Combining the strategies outlined in this book can help you build the business of your dreams even if you're struggling with chronic pain. More than building the business of your dreams, it can help you build the kind of life that you want to live.

We talked about a number of strategies to help you make that happen and that started with simplifying your business. Running a complicated business is not a badge of honor, it is a way to create additional stress and pain in your life.

Simplifying and really getting intentional about what you do in the world can be a game-changer.

Greg McKeown's *Essentialism* is a great resource to help you shift your mindset around what constitutes acceptable complication and start your journey toward simplifying. He also has a podcast to help people do that and it's worth having to listen. Another great resource is *Company of One* by Paul Jarvis, which while its approach focuses on making solopreneurship more sustainable, it really challenges and invites the readers to clarify their own values around growth to avoid growth for its own sake.

When you take time to figure out what you value, simplifying the process to get there is easier. I think we make things more complicated than they need to be when we aren't sure where we're going, what we're doing, or the best way to get there. So, we try all sorts of things in order to make sure we reach our goal wall and waste a lot of energy, time, and money in the process.

One of the paths to simplicity is around building systems. Systems help you keep things simple. They remove decision points and create a flow around how you do business. They create consistency, and a standardized way of delivering on your promises to your clients.

It isn't enough to establish systems; we also have to document them. It also allows us to put ourselves on autopilot when we aren't feeling well because we will have a system and a process to follow. There's no more trying to figure out what to do next, you have systems in place that guide your activities and you can allow the habit of following those systems to carry you through when you don't feel strong because you're in pain. That documentation facilitates our ability to bring in other people into our world and let them help us.

With those systems in place we can delegate effectively. We can stop doing everything ourselves so we can grow, find time to take care of ourselves and spend more time in our zone of genius. Effective delegation is what happens when the right people are asked to do the right thing at the right time.

Sometimes we have to let go of our need to be in control in order to help us let go of the reality that perpetuates our pain cycles. Focusing on the outcome instead of the process can be helpful for letting go of the need to control everything. When we can make peace with asking for help, it can be easier to let people into our world, into our business, and into our lives.

Running a one-person show is fine if that's what you want to do. But getting help can be a good insurance policy for when you aren't feeling well. Having a team means that your business can continue even when you're not well enough to participate. When you give them all the tools, they need to succeed without you, you can really step into your role as CEO and not be responsible for the execution of all of the things.

Having chronic pain can feel overwhelming and you can feel a certain way about what you bring to the table and how competitive your business is. When we change how we think about our challenges, it gives us more room to grow and market ourselves. The reality is, the things that we think are shameful or disappointing can be "on ramps" for people to understand us better.

Leaving space to invite people into our experience secures grace from clients by creating reciprocity in sharing our challenges. People come to us with problems that we can solve, and it can be helpful for them to know that we are people with problems too. It humanizes us and leaves common ground for relationship building.

By finding a market that doesn't care about our limitations, creating processes that don't need what we don't have, and reframing those weaknesses as strengths, we can change how we and others perceive our business and our value. It's all a matter of perspective and sometimes it just needs to shift to create space for a better experience.

The truth is that we take care of things we value and that creating that value in ourselves lends itself to better self-care. Self-care isn't just bubble baths, it's also about boundaries. Those boundaries can be with ourselves, others, they can be used to conserve our energy, and protect our time. It can also be as simple as taking care of your basic medical needs. It can be tempting to let those things slide when you're busy building a business, but when you're able to show up as your best self, you can get more done.

You are your best business asset and you need to take care of yourself. I often explain it as "you wouldn't tie your laptop to a bumper and drive it around town. That's a business tool that you need to do your job. When we let go of what we need to do to take care of ourselves we are essentially tying ourselves to our own bumpers and dragging ourselves around."

You can't pour from an empty cup and business is ultimately about serving people. We need to practice good self-care so that we can show up as the best service providers and businesspeople that we can. When you value yourself, you can charge what you're worth and have the resources that you need to take care of yourself.

One of the ways that we can practice self-care is through exercising self-compassion. I often encourage people to approach self-compassion by considering the things that you're struggling with and looking at what you would suggest to a friend.

If someone came to you and said they were struggling with pain and getting things done in their business, you wouldn't berate them or make them feel bad about what they're doing. When you're struggling with pain, being your own best friend is important and giving yourself the feedback that you would give to someone that you care about is really key.

Ultimately "shoulding" on yourself creates guilt and shame and often we are working really hard to make things happen for ourselves. The more we can give ourselves the kind of grace that we could send other people in our lives the better we can feel about the efforts that we are making.

If you're reading this book, it means that you take your business seriously and that you're trying to figure out the best way to make things happen in your business while you're dealing with pain. Congratulations!

Finding what works for you is a matter of trial and error and if you beat yourself up every time you get it wrong, you're going to have a bad time. You need to exercise self-compassion in order to be able to innovate better solutions for yourself and for your clients. Being able to accept failure and bounce back. It's about building resilience and we can bolster that by exercising self-compassion.

Pain is hard enough but dealing with big feelings around pain can be even harder. Finding ways to manage those emotions is so key. Whether that's therapy, coaching, journaling, exercise, whatever that looks like for you, having a strategy in place to deal with the feelings that are going to come up as part of your pain is an essential piece of your survival guide.

Adding to your coping toolbox can make the journey of chronic pain more bearable. It's essential to know how to process those feelings so that you can keep moving and don't stay stuck in the negativity. Learning to process and make sense of those feelings is really helpful and sometimes having additional support can make it easier.

Just like you don't have to run your business on your own, you also don't have to deal with pain on your own. You can build a team of people around you to support you as you go through this. There are all sorts of professionals that can help you manage your feelings around your pain better and reducing the stress about feeling badly about pain can also reduce your experience of pain.

We've all seen the memes floating around the internet that encourage positivity at all costs. These sentiments negate the very real experience of living with chronic pain. The reality is that it sucks and it's important to be real about that. Pain is hard and it's not a bad thing to be oriented to the reality of that. You don't have to be in denial of what is happening in order to stay positive. You can notice the mess and continue on even though it's hard.

Maintaining a positive mindset is not about ignoring the bad stuff, it's about seeing it in context and understanding that not every day is going to be a good day, but you can approach every day in a good way. Having pain does not exclude you from the experience of joy.

Joy is accessible to all of us; we just have to be open to it and find ways to integrate it into our lives.

We can access joy through play and by finding balance. Creating that balance is a practice and it doesn't happen overnight. We need to commit ourselves to it as much as we do our practical medical care, our approach to excellence in what we do and the other things that we value in our lives. Joy is a worthy goal. The journey to it is personal and worthwhile.

Using all of these tools, you can find your own way to deal with chronic pain in your business. It's all about finding out what works for you. Your experience with pain and what helps you feel better is going to be different from somebody else's experience and care instructions. We don't need to feel bad if we need different things than other people in order to feel well. The more time we spend judging what we need, the less time and energy we have to find those things and implement them in our lives.

We aren't going to get it right the first time. The process of finding what works is largely experimental and it will evolve. What you need now is going to be different than what you need six months from now, a year from now, or ten years from now. With the evolving nature of health conditions and also the progressive nature of limitations, we may find that down the road we need more or less of the things that we need today.

Every time we find something that doesn't work, we have to keep looking for something that does. It's all about experimentation and adjusting course on your journey to finding what works for your chronic pain. This is an opportunity to be innovative just like you are in the business of your business as you navigate the best way to actually run your business and take care of yourself.

There is no one-size-fits-all approach to wellness and finding the right fit means we have to try on a lot of different things. It's like shopping for clothes, not everything is going to be appropriate for the weather that you're going to experience, not everything is going to fit right, but ultimately you still have to find something to wear. That means trying more things until you find something that works.

Making that change can be scary. Change can be scary even when it's positive change. Teri Holland talked about assessing the cost of not changing and that's something that we should all do when we consider how scary it is to make a change.

The way we set up our business served a purpose for a time but if you're looking for guidance on the best way to manage your chronic pain it's probably because something isn't working. Letting go of something that doesn't serve any more is a principle that organizing expert Marie Kondo advocates for dealing with our possessions and it's also a helpful approach to dealing with our mindset, our attitude on the way we approach life.

Change can be scary, but change can be good. Implementing changes into our business allows us to be flexible with what life throws at us and it keeps us growing and learning and open to new things. Nothing stays the same forever, not even pain. The conditions that we exist in will change too. We have to be able to change with them.

Conclusion

Over the course of the pandemic, I reshaped my business to fit me better. I have been dealing with the pain of Ehlers-Danlos Syndrome and it's really challenging. The way my business was set up was not advantageous. I was doing things that my body was not happy with and I was using processes that were not kind to my limitations.

The first thing I did was I simplified my business, I shut down business lines that we're not making me enough money and that didn't make sense in the context of my overall business. I developed standard ways of delivering things to make those processes easier. Not only did I simplify what I was selling, but I simplified to whom I was selling.

Trying to develop marketing that appeals to everyone is really challenging and it's not always effective. When I had a clearer picture of who I was selling to, I was able to write copy that appealed to them and would help them sign on. Adding to that simplifying offers when they did want to sign on it was easier for them to understand what they were signing on to and to sign the dotted line.

I made peace with delegating and hired some help. I was strategic about what I delegated, and I found ways to explain what I needed so that my service providers could help me in the way that I needed to be helped.

This book was a product of me delegating and asking for help. I hired out the transcription for this book to make the process of assembling it easier. I didn't rely so much on my hands when somebody else went through the interview transcripts and made grabbing quotes easier.

I didn't just ask for help professionally but I also did personally. I hired a housekeeper to help me with the house. I outsourced meal preparation because it's something I didn't enjoy and that I found uncomfortable with my pain. I did everything I could to free up what energy I had and direct it where I needed it, my business.

I hired a therapist to help me work through the big feelings that came with the pandemic, becoming a single mom, growing a business during a global health crisis, and also writing a book at the same time. Her insights were invaluable.

I hired coaches to help me with my fat loss goals so that I could feel better with less pressure on my joints. I hired a massage therapist to help me deal with the pain and muscle tension that comes with my condition.

I also did the boring things, such as order my pain medication and take it as directed, and use my CPAP so that I would get proper sleep. I was given an exercise bike so that I could work out without having to worry about going to a gym where I could be exposed to the virus.

I started ordering myself bath bombs because as much as self-care isn't just about bubble baths it can also include them. It was also a great way for me to support another business owner who struggles with chronic pain herself.

The gratitude practice that I started over the pandemic helped me reframe what was happening and focus on the good things that were coming to light. And such an objectively difficult situation, it's easy to not feel grateful. But that gratitude went a long way to helping me make the best of a difficult situation.

I found ways to play and explore joy. I went back to dance class even though it was something I was nervous to do. I was afraid I would dislocate things.

I also experimented with movement privately. One night I just put on music and danced around my living room and it was so freeing. I realized that I didn't need somebody to teach me how to dance. I just needed to give myself permission to play in that way. At a time where I was struggling with feeling like there wasn't enough play in my life, that moving exploration made a big difference.

I started really focusing on curating experiences for myself and also on how I wanted to feel and what I needed to do to feel that way. I surrounded myself with people who are supportive, encouraging, and who indulged my love of life and helped me remember who I am.

I started this process feeling like I had lost everything, and I didn't have a direction. I had been running my business for three and a half years and it was keeping the lights on, but it was incredibly stressful trying to make ends meet. By streamlining my offer and who I sold to, I was able to sell more things and create more peace in my life by resourcing my family more effectively.

It took trial and error and a lot of error to find the process that works for me and I had to exercise a lot of self-compassion in order to get there and find the strength to keep going. It was hard continually coming up against challenges and trying solutions that didn't work. While I'm excited about how far I've come, I recognize that this is a work in progress and I will always be adjusting these things and finding new ways to innovate, increase profitability, create more balance, and find more happiness in my life.

One of the challenges that I faced in the beginning was that I really didn't understand that things could get better. I thought what I had going on was as good as it gets. I couldn't even imagine a life where I was experiencing less pain or had more success in my business or more joy. I was feeling limited, but the limit was actually my own imagination. It wasn't just a fear of dreaming bigger, it was literally not knowing what those dreams could be.

What I wish I knew

I wish I knew before how much better I could feel if I took care of myself. I wish I knew before how much easier it would be if I focused and niched down and dialed in on my zone of genius. I wish I knew it was possible to make more money and to be happier and to live a life that was radically different from anything I've ever known before and be OK with it.

I wish I knew that I could do this because it would have made it so much easier. But having gone through this process of living through this pandemic and building my business, online schooling my child, and navigating single motherhood, I feel confident to face any of life's challenges ahead.

My resilience was built in a time of sourdough and sadness. But I didn't do it alone.

I wish I knew that when I faced hard times and that my community would hold me because this book would not have happened without my community. This has been a patchwork quilt of love and encouragement sent from the people that I love to help others navigate their pain journey. I wrote the book, but it has been a community project to support wellness within the entrepreneurial landscape.

My life is radically different now and yours can be too. I didn't have any special skills that made me uniquely qualified to navigate this journey that made me better able to do it than anyone else. I took my brave and I applied it to a difficult time, and I came out further ahead than I expected.

I decided I deserved an extraordinary life and I decided to go for it. You deserve to have one too. You deserve better than working yourself to exhaustion for not enough money, feeling alone and disconnected from your people, and struggling with discouragement. You deserve better and you can have better if you get intentional about what you want and give yourself the space that you need to try something different.

Your mileage may vary but when you take the time to build something that works for you instead of trying to cram yourself into a box that doesn't fit you, you can experience more satisfaction, more comfort, and more joy. You can create your ideal day, find ways to deal with the big feelings that come up, and better ways to take care of your mind, body, and soul.

If somebody had told me back in January of 2020 that by the end of the year I would write a book, significantly increase my visibility, grow my community and my bank account, and find more comfort in my body than I ever have, I wouldn't have believed them.

While I have my own skills and abilities, I'm not particularly special as far as pain management skill goes and this is something that anybody can do.

Your pain might be chronic, but your profits can be too. Create your own road map with the principles we've discussed and find your own way to the destination of your choosing. I can't wait to see where you go!

Laws may change frequently or without notice. The information in this book may be updated from time to time as things change, or to ensure compliance with laws and regulations. Please type the URL below into a web browser to check for updates, and always verify information independently.

IMPORTANT

www.self-counsel.com/updates/chronicprofit/check21.html

OTHER TITLES OF INTEREST FROM SELF-COUNSEL PRESS

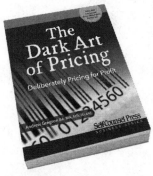

The Dark Art of Pricing
Deliberately Pricing for Profit

Andrew Gregson, BA, MA, MSc (Economics)
ISBN: 978-1-77040-315-4
$21.95 USD/$29.95 CAD

For many business owners, the process of determining how to price products or services is akin to boiling eye of newt in a cauldron surrounded by wicked witches. But pricing is not magic, any more than selling is magic. *The Dark Art of Pricing* demystifies pricing for small- to medium-sized businesses.

Pricing should be of the utmost importance to business owners because it is possible to use price strategies to engineer a deliberate profit. It is possible to drive sales and cut costs. An accountant can tell you how to cut costs. Sales trainers can help you improve sales. But what is often mostly ignored is pricing, and focusing on price allows you to find that sweet spot where you become the price leader because you are the best in your industry or area, and the go-to company because of the value you offer.

Finding the right pricing strategy is like developing a sales program: work. It takes testing and tweaking. But the "how" and "why" are buried in corporate vaults and academic journals, almost inaccessible to the average business owner. Author Andrew Gregson has started and owned five businesses including two franchises, and spent years consulting on profitability to small- and medium-sized businesses in North America. He simplifies the strategies that help business owners find ways to charge what they are really worth, drive larger profits, build wealth, and eventually attract buyers when the time comes to retire to a sandy beach.

The exclusive downloadable kit included with the book contains:

- Worksheets from the book
- Resources to help you in pricing your products or services

Managing Remote Staff
Capitalize on Work-from-Home Productivity
Lin Grensing-Pophal, SPHR, SHRM-SCP, PCM
ISBN: 978-1-77040-331-4
$19.95 USD/$26.95 CAD

The world as we know it has changed. Even businesses that long ago declared that working from home wasn't an option have found themselves adjusting and overhauling their business models, since the only other alternative is to close.

Despite being thrust into this "new normal," businesses and their displaced staff have risen to the challenges and acclimatized to ways of working remotely. Since then, the idea of managing remote workers has grown and become more widely accepted as a viable way to do business.

If your business needs more employees but you don't have the office space to accommodate them; someone on your staff wants to work from home; you want to promote a flexible work environment but fear losing profits; or you simply need to adapt due to a pandemic as so many have had to do, managing remote staff may be the answer.

Managing Remote Staff: Capitalize on Work-from-Home Productivity explains how to:

- Determine whether remote staffing is right for your company
- Assess new and current candidates
- Train managers and employees remotely
- Help at-home or off-site staff to cope
- Set up a home office
- Measure the success of your program
- Take care of the legal details

This book provides managers with the tools to set up and maintain a productive remote staffing program that benefits both employees and employers.